REINVENTION

REINVENTION

THE PROMISE
AND CHALLENGE
OF TRANSFORMING
A COMMUNITY
COLLEGE SYSTEM

Cheryl L. Hyman

HARVARD EDUCATION PRESS
CAMBRIDGE, MASSACHUSETTS

Paperback ISBN 978-1-68253-192-1
Library Edition ISBN 978-1-68253-193-8

Library of Congress Cataloging-in-Publication Data
Names: Hyman, Cheryl L., author.
Title: Reinvention : the promise and challenge of transforming a community college system / Cheryl L. Hyman.
Description: Cambridge, Massachusetts : Harvard Education Press, 2018. | Includes bibliographical references and index.
Identifiers: LCCN 2017060935| ISBN 9781682531921 (pbk.) | ISBN 9781682531938 (library edition)
Subjects: LCSH: Community colleges—Illinois—Chicago. | Community colleges—Illinois—Chicago—Administration. | Community colleges—Illinois—Chicago—Management. | City Colleges of Chicago. | City Colleges of Chicago—Administration. | City Colleges of Chicago—Management. | Educational change—Illinois—Chicago.
Classification: LCC LB2328 .H96 2018 | DDC 378.1/5430977311—dc23 LC record available at https://lccn.loc.gov/2017060935

Published by Harvard Education Press,
an imprint of the Harvard Education Publishing Group

Harvard Education Press
8 Story Street
Cambridge, MA 02138

Cover Design: Wilcox Design
The typefaces used in this book are ITC Slimbach, TT Prosto Sans, and Milo.

There are four women that have gone on to reside in what I believe to be a much better place

Granny Payne, Granny Hyman, Granny Norsworthy, and Mother Doris

Whom I know continue to watch over me with great pride and everlasting love.

and

To Lorraine, my guardian angel on earth, who sticks with me until I'm unstuck!!!!!

Contents

CONTENTS

FOREWORD

When in 2010 I first heard that Mayor Richard M. Daley had appointed a businessperson to be the next chancellor of the City Colleges of Chicago, I was intrigued. I had been part of earlier efforts by community and advocacy groups in Chicago to convince the mayor to focus more attention on improving the City Colleges. His tapping Cheryl Hyman—an experienced leader from the private sector with no experience in college administration—indicated that he was willing (finally) to do something to shake up Chicago's community colleges.

But I was also skeptical. I had worked with the City Colleges, community organizations, and employers starting in the mid-1990s to develop "adult technical bridge" programs, a sort of boot camp designed to prepare adults with poor education or limited English skills to enter college-level, career-technical training programs that would in turn lead to career-path technician jobs in manufacturing, health care, information technology, and other fields. These efforts created a successful model that has since been replicated throughout the country.

In my work with the City Colleges, I observed that, like a lot of community colleges, the institution was very focused on inputs—on getting students into classes—and not much on outcomes—ensuring that they completed with degrees of value for employment and further education. This preoccupation with access over success showed in the results: graduation rates were in the single digits. Many occupational programs were outdated and failed to train students for jobs in demand.

Not surprisingly, then, the City Colleges of Chicago were held in low regard by employers and universities. And they were not respected by community organizations and the Chicago Public Schools (CPS), even though they offered adult literacy programs through many community-based organizations, and were and still are the most common destination for CPS graduates who go on to college.

Although I worked with some excellent faculty, staff, and administrators, management of the colleges was not generally strong. In the several years I partnered with the colleges, I never saw a broad-based effort to engage faculty, advisers, and others in efforts to design improvements in programs and support services. Faculty and staff were rarely, if ever, shown data on how students were faring at the colleges outside of individual classes, much less what happened to them after they left. The result was a culture that was unaccustomed to innovation—and in many respects, resistant to it.

Another source of my skepticism was that there was no clear guidance in the field about how to turn around a large community college system (or even a small college, for that matter). Since the early 2000s, there had been a great ferment of activity in community colleges nationally aimed at improving student outcomes. Achieving the Dream, funded by Lumina and many other foundations and involving over 150 colleges nationally, is one prominent example. Yet research we at the Community College Research Center and others conducted on these reforms found that the programs tended to be relatively small in scale and that their positive effects diminished over time. While in many cases, they benefited small numbers of students, they were not succeeding in moving the needle on student completion rates overall or reducing equity gaps in achievement between students by race and income. This led to a growing recognition among researchers and practitioners that to improve student outcomes substantially, "boutique" innovations would not suffice; rather, colleges needed to fundamentally redesign their programs and support services. The field had some high-performing colleges that had achieved standards of excellence to strive for, but there was no "playbook" on how to turn around a system as poorly performing as Chicago's City Colleges.

In this candid and provocative book, Cheryl Hyman chronicles the efforts she led at the City Colleges to address these obstacles: challenging the culture of complacency that sometimes characterizes colleges and engaging faculty and administrators around a far-reaching and comprehensive program of reform.

I had the good fortune to observe these efforts by Hyman and her team, serving as a pro bono adviser to the whole-system redesign—the "City College Reinvention." From this experience, I saw that that her approach to the work was animated by a set of core ideas—ideas that reflected her personal and professional experience.

The first was that a student-centered education needs to be a *career-focused* one. Hyman calls this principle *relevance*: what students are taught needs to be relevant to what they hope to achieve. Hyman believes that what students and their families are seeking foremost when they invest the time, money, and effort to go to college is entrée to a career. It was her own desire to have a professional job in an office downtown, along with an interest in computers, that motivated Hyman to earn a college degree and thereby escape a life of poverty.

As Hyman points out in this book, the debate about the purpose of a community college education has been going on since the first community college, Joliet Junior College, was established in 1901—a debate that unfortunately has been driven by class and racial conflict. Chicago's City Colleges themselves evolved from post–high school courses first taught in 1911 at two Chicago vocational high schools, which later added general education and prep-professional focuses to the "terminal" vocational programs. As has been true in community colleges nationally, these three mission areas were never reconciled with one another.

Hyman emphatically rejects this separation. She believes that to thrive in today's workplace and society, students need both the broad skills of the sort associated with the liberal arts *and* strong technical skills. They also need degrees—and increasingly, bachelor's degrees even in occupations that traditionally did not require a baccalaureate. This is supported by research on the returns to postsecondary credentials. Hyman advocates a "third way" that integrates academic and vocational education. She urged her colleagues at the City Colleges to move out of their traditional organizational siloes because their students suffer as a result. Students taking general education arts and sciences courses need to see the connection of these courses to careers of interest to them, while those in career programs need broader skills and college degrees if they are be able to advance in their careers. While faculty may be reluctant to embrace this view, students and their families clearly understand this, which is reflected in continued demand for "degrees with skills."

A second idea underlying Hyman's approach to reinventing the City Colleges is the efficacy of applying business practices to running educational institutions. She and her team used private-sector know-how to improve operational competence and fiscal efficiency—both of which had been sorely lacking at the City Colleges before she came. Today, when states continue to cut subsidies for public higher education and colleges are forced to rely more and more on tuition—while trying to keep costs affordable to students and their families—sound fiscal management is increasingly essential for the survival of public colleges and universities. Hyman saved tens of millions of dollars by streamlining administration and business processes, savings that were reinvested in the educational programs and student support services of the colleges.

Hyman's experience in business taught her more than just how to run an efficient operation. As she describes in the book, when she was at Commonwealth Edison, Hyman led a team that introduced major innovations, increased efficiencies, and supported improved operations. A key lesson she brought with her to the City Colleges is that to effect fundamental change in practice, it is necessary to change the culture. To do that, you have to change hearts and minds. Hyman's strategy for changing attitudes at the City Colleges was to broadly engage her colleagues in redesigning their institution. In late 2010, she invited people from throughout the colleges, in all types of roles from faculty to IT staff, to join Reinvention task forces that would spend an entire semester working together to make recommendations for reform on issues from program portfolio to faculty and staff development and technology. Once a task force came up with a solution, they were responsible for conducting workshops to present their ideas to other colleagues and solicit further input. Later, each college set up separate task forces to further deepen engagement. Ultimately, over 20 percent of full-time faculty, in addition to many staff and administrators, were directly involved in the process, which resulted in changes in practice I would not have thought possible when I worked with the City Colleges several years before.

The third essential idea behind Hyman's approach is the overriding importance of accountability both to students and to taxpayers. She acknowledges that community colleges are poorly funded (all the more reason why a focus on fiscal efficiency is important). She recognizes that many City Colleges students come unprepared academically and that many have fraught lives outside of school where even getting by day to day can be a challenge. So there are lots of reasons the community college mission is not easy to fulfill. Yet, the hand Hyman was dealt in her own life was far from ideal. She could have made a lot of excuses for not trying to make a better life. And once she'd made it in the private sector, she could have continued with a lucrative career. But she wanted to give back. These values formed through her own life were manifest in how she approached leading the City Colleges. Every time I saw her speak publicly, she communicated a clear message: *The City Colleges' job is to serve the students who come to them, and we are accountable to students and taxpayers for doing so. There are lots of obstacles, but we're in this business for a reason. No one else will do this if colleges won't. The mission is so important that we cannot make excuses.*

Cheryl's thinking along these lines turns out to have been very prescient. By following these guiding ideas, Hyman and her colleagues at the City Colleges conceived and implemented innovations in practice that have begun only in the past two or three years to take hold in the community college landscape nationally. These include working with employers and university partners to more clearly map programs to career-path jobs and further education, requiring all students to select a broad field and develop a full-program plan in their first term, and implementing technology systems to allow advisers and students themselves to monitor progress along their plans and change course as needed.

Now that reforms along these lines are sweeping the field, *Reinvention: The Promise and Challenge of Transforming a Community College System* is quite timely. It tells the story about the innovative in practice that the City Colleges put in place, and how they managed the change process. *Reinvention* is the playbook for redesigning a large urban college system that was missing from the field when Hyman came to the City Colleges in in 2010.

The changes in practice the City Colleges implemented under Hyman's leadership were pathbreaking and enabled the colleges to substantially improve outcomes for students. However, the extent to which the field is successful in adopting similar reforms will depend less on what specific practices colleges put in place, but rather on whether college leaders can change mindsets. We will not see sustained reform until faculty, staff, and administrators adopt the guiding ideas manifested in Hyman's leadership. We need to move beyond the antiquated academic-vocational divide and see that in today's world, both as workers and citizens, our students will need broad skills and technical ones, and that increasingly, a bachelor's degree (ideally with certificates and associate degrees embedded) is required for career-path employment. We have to accept that in order to provide a quality education with limited resources, colleges have much to learn from the private sector both in terms of operational and fiscal management and in how to manage large-scale change. Finally, we need to recommit ourselves to our students and the vital public role of community colleges. We must hold ourselves and our students to high standards—and be accountable to students and taxpayers for doing so.

In this book, Hyman shows us how to this. As she makes clear, if we don't do it, no one else will. It is up to us. There are no excuses.

Davis Jenkins
Senior Research Scholar, Community College Research Center
Teachers College, Columbia University

CHAPTER 1

THE CALL

"I Need You to Fix It"

One winter day in 2009, I was contacted by an influential African American businessman, without whose support little happens in Chicago. "You're going to get a phone call soon," he told me, "and you should just say yes."

A few weeks later, the phone rang on my desk at Commonwealth Edison, the Chicago-based *Fortune* 500 company where I served as vice president for operations strategy and business intelligence. A woman's voice announced, "The mayor wants to meet with you."

Having once been a lobbyist for ComEd, it wasn't uncommon for me to speak with mayors—suburban mayors. But I had no idea what this was about.

"Which mayor?" I asked.

"Mayor Daley."

I thought I was being pranked. Though I was a vice president at one of the largest public utilities in the nation, I had never spoken with the city's longtime mayor, Richard M. Daley—and had no reason to do so. That was a job for my boss, John Hooker.

I asked John if he knew what this was about. The mayor was vetting me, he said, as a potential candidate to run the city's community college system.

This took me by surprise. I was doing well where I was and puzzled at why this would be a good match. City Colleges was a massive, century-old system of seven community colleges educating more than 100,000 students each year in the city where I'd lived all my life. Even though I had attended one of those colleges, Olive-Harvey, twenty-five years earlier, I knew almost nothing about the system. I had no background in education, nor did I know much about community colleges in general.

But I knew that education meant everything to me, that City Colleges gave me my start in life, and that I was going to hear the mayor out.

● ● ●

This book is my attempt to chart a way forward for community colleges, institutions that should and could serve more fully as a vector of social advancement and economic empowerment for all Americans. It offers a blunt assessment: We must break old habits so that our colleges are organized not around old habits and old misconceptions, but rather around the dreams and needs of the students and society they are meant to serve. This book chronicles the advances of one effort that led to rapid improvement of key student success measures and to a more solid tethering of community colleges to employers and four-year institutions. But it also shines a harsh light on the challenges that accompany that progress, some of which we could not overcome. The story of the massive institutional reform we called Reinvention at City Colleges of Chicago illuminates lessons learned for the many others who are tackling the high-stakes task of making our community colleges more responsive to society's needs.

US community colleges educate about 10 million people a year—38 percent of the nation's undergraduates.[1] What that education looks like varies widely. Some community college students seek a credential that will immediately launch them into a career, like dental hygiene or welding. For others, like me, an associate degree from a community college is the first step toward a four-year bachelor's degree, and then perhaps further education. Employers send workers to community college to train in new skills, immigrants attend to learn English and to further their education, and people who didn't complete high school come to get a GED.

In 1973, fewer than 7 percent of eighteen- to twenty-four-year-olds receiving postsecondary education in the United States were registered at a community college. Forty years later, as more jobs required a higher level of education, the percentage had almost doubled, to nearly 13 percent.[2] The growth has especially benefited Americans who have been disadvantaged. Although some programs are selective, community colleges are open-access, relatively low-cost institutions, and for many students they provide the only possible path to a degree of value. Not only have students relied on community colleges as a gateway to opportunity, employers have depended on them to provide skilled workers.

But this interdependence has a precondition: that entering community college leads to a degree, and that that degree leads to a good-paying job. When I began doing research to decide whether I might want to play a role at City Colleges, I learned very quickly that this was not the way things were working out—neither in Chicago nor in many other places in America.

• • •

At ComEd, I was used to analyzing outcomes. To prepare for the meeting with Mayor Daley, I went to the City Colleges website to look up data about the institution's performance. I found almost nothing. I did learn that my alma mater, Olive-Harvey College on the city's far South Side, was part of a system with six other community colleges across Chicago—a fact, it would turn out, that was unknown to many students who attended the institution. It didn't matter per se that the students didn't know the colleges' names. What would come to bother me was that it was a sign that students were not exposed to the full array of options the system offered, and because of that, they might limit themselves to opportunities just around the corner from their house.

I would also learn that enrollment at City Colleges had dropped 30 percent over the previous decade. I didn't know that only 30 percent of first-time full-time students at US community colleges earned a degree within three years of enrolling, or that the average community college graduation rate in the ten biggest US cities was 16 percent, or that at City

Colleges, it was an atrocious 7 percent. In a system with nearly fifty-eight thousand associate degree students, only about two thousand got a degree each year. Few of the students who entered City Colleges with plans to eventually earn a bachelor's degree actually did so. Fifty-four percent of degree-seeking students dropped out in their first six months. Of the forty thousand adult education students who sought GEDs or studied English as a second language, only 35 percent met their personal goals each year, and only five hundred transitioned to college-credit programs, a must in today's economy.[3]

As I would come to learn more about the institution, I discovered more alarming statistics. By 2018, 64 percent of jobs in Illinois would require some postsecondary education, jobs requiring associate degrees were projected to grow at double the rate of those that required no college, and 1.5 million jobs would require an associate degree.[4]

That one of the nation's largest community college systems wasn't poised to meet these challenges was no secret to a small group of civic leaders who had been insisting to Mayor Daley that if City Colleges didn't significantly improve, Chicago employers would never be able to fill middle-skills jobs. Working in consultation with the Office of the Mayor, a group of civic, corporate, nonprofit, foundation, and education leaders brought together by Chicago's Civic Consulting Alliance began to examine the impact of City Colleges of Chicago and discuss what was needed for the system to truly benefit students, and the city.

Not only were students highly unlikely to complete their programs at City College, if they did there was little indication that they were prepared for employment, much less employment in high-demand fields. The group looked at labor market data that showed which industries would create the most jobs in coming years—and it was little surprise when a cursory review of City Colleges programs showed a mismatch between the skills being taught and what the region was looking for. Few employers had even heard of the city's community colleges. City Colleges still taught the same computer programming language I had learned at Olive-Harvey a quarter-century earlier, and some four-year institutions refused to accept certain City College credits. This painted a dire picture for City Colleges of Chicago. It was extremely heartbreaking to me, given this was the place that gave me and so many others a start in college.

The Civic Consulting Alliance concluded that change was imperative. "For the sake of our employers; for our city's overall economic health; and most importantly, for the sake of those residents who have been left out of opportunity for too long, we can, and must, use this asset more effectively," the group's members wrote in a 2007 report.[5] As I learned from Brian Fabes—a former McKinsey executive and university faculty member and administrator who had convened both the original group meeting with Mayor Daley before I became chancellor and the first group meeting I held as chancellor—because City Colleges didn't closely monitor data about student outcomes, and because officials were reluctant to share what little information did exist, it was hard for the group to gauge exactly where the problems originated and whether the City Colleges were positioned to rise to the challenge.[6] But they saw potential—and a critical need—for the institution to do so. The system was large and relatively well resourced. And, unlike in other large cities, it (like many other Chicago education and workforce agencies) reported directly to the mayor. If the mayor really wanted improvement, he could put his full force behind making it happen.

Mayor Daley, whose father, Richard J. Daley, had served as Chicago mayor for twenty-one years and for whom one of the seven City Colleges was named, was indeed passionate about reforming City Colleges. It was imperative, he would later tell me, to keep Chicago globally competitive, to give as many Chicagoans as possible a shot at reaching and staying in the middle class, and to use education to address the challenge of violence in the city—because we believed, like so many others, that a paycheck is the best alternative to a gun.

Daley understood that his efforts to reform the Chicago Public Schools would not make a big difference if high school graduates didn't have a solid option for college; it would do little good to remove one barrier if a taller one stood right behind it. "More than ever," he wrote in a City Colleges publication, "a skilled workforce is necessary to compete in the global economy and to bring the knowledge- and technology-based jobs of the twenty-first century to our city. If our entire education system does not produce that workforce, we can't compete. It is as simple as that."[7]

Daley decided that when the opportunity arose to appoint a new chancellor, he wanted him or her to come from outside education. One person he asked for suggestions was then–ComEd CEO Frank Clark. The mayor told Clark he wanted a businessperson who would work with educators to apply strategic management principles to the system's challenges. And he wanted someone who had walked in the students' shoes.

• • •

If you go by statistics and societal expectations, I was not supposed to be a corporate vice president—or a candidate to lead one of the country's largest higher education institutions. I grew up in the Henry Horner Homes housing project, a place so plagued by negative stereotypes that a 1987 *New York Times* article about it was titled "What It's Like to Be in Hell."[8] The complex had been built in the 1950s by Richard J. Daley but had been recently torn down by his son in an attempt to break the cycle of poverty and violence that plagued it. In actuality, life was comfortable and pleasant for me there. I was surrounded by a community that shared responsibility for its children. My parents had good middle-class jobs—my dad at the phone company and my mom at a bank. But when I was ten, my parents divorced, then both began to struggle with substance abuse. They eventually overcame the cycle, but not before it had taken a toll on our financial and emotional footing as a family. When I was sixteen, I dropped out of high school, filled a garbage bag with my belongings, and left home for the streets. The streets sometimes felt more stable than home, which was not saying much. Even with the precarious conditions there, I was fortunate to have a guardian angel guiding me to rough but caring people who had spent their life learning how to survive in this environment and somehow found the means to take care of themselves and the compassion to look out for me. I watched as friends became addicts, committed crimes, and died violent deaths. Those of us who didn't die were just fading away.

Yet somehow, even as I was trying to survive, I knew I belonged downtown instead, with a briefcase and a suit, or in an elegant dress with stylish shoes. I just had no earthly clue how to get there. My street family, especially two older mentors, advised me to go back to school. For them, it was more than advice. It was a way for them to attain some form of victory, despite their own mistakes. They felt their chance had passed, but I still had time. They scrounged up some money—I did not ask too many questions—to help me buy books. At age seventeen, I went back to high school and moved in with a friend's mother. Thanks to a job at Kentucky Fried Chicken, I met my basic needs, just barely.

I got my diploma in 1986, then, captivated by TV ads that promised a quick road to a profitable computer career, I enrolled in a for-profit "college." Thousands of dollars and six months later, the trade school, as it was called then, delivered me not a career downtown with a briefcase or fancy shoes but rather a drawerful of useless certificates that didn't even lead to a job. I had only learned to use WordPerfect—and one other important thing: I didn't just want to work with computers, I wanted to *make* them work. I also learned that shortcuts are shortsighted and often lead to dead ends. I set my sights on the Illinois Institute of Technology (IIT), but it was out of reach both academically and financially. I was lugging around a $2,500 student loan like a ball and chain, with earning potential of, at best, a fast-food wage of $3.35 an hour.

I needed help, emotionally, financially, and spiritually. One day, I broke down and, in a heart-to-heart that broke her heart, I told my grandmother about everything: my parents' struggles, the streets, the bogus certificates, the debt. She had had a career as a nurse after attending Malcolm X College, one of the City Colleges of Chicago, and recommended the institution to me. Soon after, I walked into Olive-Harvey College and asked how to register for classes.

I was badly prepared academically, but thanks to dogged determination and the persistent help of two kind, dedicated professors, I went from a D to an A in algebra in the span of one semester. There is no shame in D's; the trick is to rebound from them. Eventually, I proudly graduated and received my associate degree with almost straight A's in my last semester, and was finally accepted at IIT. After getting my bachelor's in computer science in 1996, I got a systems analyst job at ComEd. But I never stopped learning. I earned a master's in community development with a certification in nonprofit management from North Park University and an executive MBA from Northwestern University's Kellogg School of Business.

Along the way, I climbed the corporate ladder at ComEd, from IT specialist to analyst to lobbyist to vice president. I was involved in a wide variety of projects, from designing and coding processes for nuclear and fossil stations to creating disaster recovery plans to identifying philanthropic investments for the company to streamlining processes and enhancing customer service processes.

That I would even consider a public-sector job—and its relatively low benefits compared with the corporate world—puzzled some of my corporate colleagues. But for me, a chancellor's salary was still far beyond anything I could have dreamed of as I studied in my car under streetlights not that long ago. In addition, I had come to see that my years in the corporate world had met my intellectual and material needs, but had left an emotional void. I always thought it was my destiny to right wrongs—even as a child, I had written a letter to President Reagan scolding him for increased bus fares (though I learned, thirty years later, that my parents never mailed it). Years earlier, in an effort to contribute, I had applied to teach at Olive-Harvey, though my application disappeared into a void. The more I learned about what City Colleges students weren't getting from their education, the more I wanted to change that.

• • •

Even though I had been a lobbyist, I never had such a high-stakes conversation with such a powerful politician. As I took the elevator to "the Fifth Floor"—shorthand in Chicago for the mayor's office—I couldn't help but wonder why Daley was interested in me leading City Colleges. But from the start, the mayor seemed impressed by my background. He knew my story and believed it mattered: a homeless high school dropout who, thanks to the community college system, found her way back and grew into an accomplished business executive.

Daley may have had a special reason to seek out a chancellor from ComEd leadership. In July 1995, a heat wave engulfed Chicago, with temperatures up to 106 degrees and extreme humidity. Power outages exacerbated the problem at a time air-conditioning was critical. Throughout what the medical examiner described as "a disaster like we've never seen in the city of Chicago," which resulted in a significant number of deaths, ComEd's performance raised serious concerns—and even rage—among the public, media, and elected officials. In addition, in the summer of 1999, a glitch at ComEd caused a blackout of the Chicago loop that lasted for several days and attracted national and international attention. Mayor Daley's reaction to this episode was, to say the least, explosive. He demanded ComEd should start firing some its top executives.

John Rowe, CEO of Exelon (ComEd's parent company) had just returned to Chicago to lead the utility but took full responsibility for the company's failure, including discharging the company's senior engineer at that time. A decade and more than $1 billion in investments later, he and other leaders at ComEd and Exelon had completely turned around their operations, reliability, and public image. Daley had faith that an executive from a company that had managed such an impressive transformation could turn around the community college system as well.

I knew going into my meeting that if I were chancellor, my single-minded focus would be to ensure that a City Colleges education would ultimately make a student better off. These students needed to get a degree that counted for something—and get it in a timely manner. This was what the mayor wanted too, and he appreciated the forthrightness he knew I would bring to the task. I had always been told I had tough elbows. People said this as if it was something to apologize for. Not Daley. "People say you're pretty tough," he told me. "Good. This is not about making friends." The colleges, Daley said, seem to be focused on what everyone needs—but not enough on what students need to compete in todays economy: "Somebody needs to fix it. I need you to fix it."

Those were the words I had hoped to hear, but instead of being elated, I was scared. It was not that I couldn't surmount challenges—my experiences on the streets proved that I could. But having had those experiences, I knew exactly how high the stakes were for City Colleges' students. I was afraid to let them down any more than they already had been.

● ● ●

I started as chancellor in March 2010. In my first weeks, it quickly became clear that I was no longer in corporate America. The senior team was made up mostly of academics who had come up through the classroom. They clearly cared about students. They were helpful and committed, just like the people I had encountered at Olive-Harvey decades earlier. But there was a stark difference between the performance-oriented culture I had left in the corporate world and the inefficient—and, worse, complacent—culture at City Colleges.

When I gathered the vice chancellor of academic affairs, college presidents, and other senior administrators for the first time, I asked what each person did. They recited their job descriptions but couldn't speak to their goals, strategies, or results. When I asked to meet with a department head, seven people would show up. I asked someone in the meeting about the college's pass rate on the NCLEX, the professional licensure exam for nursing. "What's the NCLEX?" an administrator responded. (The pass rate was, by the way, 42 percent, half the national average and 33 points below Illinois's required threshold.) Every week, I had to sign dozens of paper time sheets, verifying that employees I had not even met had actually shown up for work.

I was not angry about this culture clash, and I did not blame anyone for what I would have seen just a few weeks before, in corporate America, as a very strange meeting and unacceptable practices. But the complacency was another matter. While every indicator showed that students were not being served, I heard a very different assessment from some of the administrators at the meeting and other employees within City Colleges. Everyone thought the institution was performing well or they had excuses for why it wasn't. I couldn't blame some of them for this perception; no one had ever really showed them detailed data that suggested anything different.

At that first leadership meeting, everyone was very solicitous, asking what they could do for me. What they could do, I said, was tell me about their student outcomes, their performance, and their budgets. I was met by blank stares. Soon, one courageous soul ventured an answer, followed by another. The students were doing well, they said. One graduate recently had come back to let everyone know she was doing well at the university, and it had been very moving. Other touching anecdotes followed. The challenge, I realized at that moment, would be to negotiate the melding of these two cultures. My team simply had the kind of outlook political scientist Kenneth Meier described in his research: "Community college practitioners, unless pressured externally by policymakers, accrediting agencies, or critics, are accustomed to rationalizing their practice by pointing to the degree of access they provide to higher education and to their good intentions . . . When pressed with evidence of marginal institutional outcomes, the practitioner's culture often responds with 'Horatio Alger stories of student success' while sidestepping the problem of contested institutional outcomes."[9]

So we learned that ten former students were on track to success. What about the other hundreds of thousands?

It was clear that the administrators and faculty cared about the institution and the students. It struck me, however, that they were quick to place the accountability for poor outcomes—insofar as they acknowledged them—on everyone but themselves. They complained that funding was a challenge, that for-profits were stealing students, and so on. There was one bit of data everyone did seem to know: nine in ten students arrived at City Colleges needed remediation in English, math, or both. The response to this was, overwhelmingly, resignation: "The students come to us so ill-prepared, what can you expect?" An administrator told me that one of the department heads had said there was not one thing he could do in the classroom to overcome the students' academic deficiencies.

There were plenty of external factors that contributed to these challenges. The lack of focus on outcomes, for instance, was a pernicious side effect of the way Illinois funded community colleges. Money was allocated based solely on enrollment, not on outcomes. Administrators were thus focused primarily on the head count that determined the size of their budgets. Paired with that reality was the common attitude that because some of our campuses are located in some of the highest crime areas in Chicago, being a relatively functional institution that provided a safe haven for students was enough.

But that attitude was beginning to change. Just before I began my job at City Colleges, President Barack Obama announced an initiative to increase the number of US college graduates by 5 million by 2020. Obama, policymakers, philanthropic foundations, and community college reformers across the country were starting to catalyze the cultivation of a new mindset, one I firmly subscribe to: *Access alone is not enough.* This growing awareness would break what I often referred to as the "silent crisis" of community colleges. We are not doing students any favors if they don't complete their degrees, and if those degrees don't make them productive citizens and lead to gainful employment.

"The rub," wrote Meier, surveying the community college landscape in the early 2000s, was that, except for a few vocational areas, "the outcomes of millions of other students, especially minorities, entering and leaving with embarrassing frequency need to be addressed forthrightly and systematically if the community college is going to achieve its historic commitments to democracy and social justice."[10]

The application of these principles at City Colleges of Chicago eventually led to a dramatic increase in the quantity and quality of credentials awarded, but it also led to significant controversy. In the months I spent learning about City Colleges, I saw that the institution had pockets of untapped potential: adequate (though poorly used) resources, intelligent faculty and administrators, a ton of space (seven colleges and six satellite sites), and a few strong-performing programs. But I also saw little proof that the colleges were reliably putting students, and the city of Chicago, on track to success. I had just spent fourteen years in the corporate world and had all sorts of management tools in my toolkit. But they would come to nothing unless we could combat the tyranny of low expectations.

CHAPTER 2

ACCESS VERSUS SUCCESS

The Case for Change

The tension over the purpose of community colleges wasn't anything new. It dated back more than a century, and had its origin, it turned out, in the Chicago area. Coming to better understand the history of the community college debate helped me understand how deep the cultural rifts ran in higher education.[1]

In the late nineteenth century, presidents at several prestigious universities, including Columbia, Stanford, the University of Michigan, and the University of Chicago, had begun expressing a desire to focus the university on research and training for the intellectual elite, and create another type of institution to educate high school graduates who, they argued, wouldn't be served by a more academically rigorous college. In 1898, William Rainey Harper, the first president of the University of Chicago, suggested that the first two years of college instruction would be best left to other institutions because "it is not until the end of the Sophomore year that university methods of instruction may be employed to advantage." Alexis Lange, dean of the school of education at the University of California, was even blunter: "The upward extension of the high school [would] be in the educational interests of the great mass of high school graduates who cannot, will not, should not, become university students."[2] These men saw "junior college" as the end of the road for the majority of those who pursued post–high school education.

Originally, Harper and his colleagues intended to split the University of Chicago into a junior and a senior college on the same campus; those who received a two-year associate degree were meant "to give up college work at the end of the sophomore year." Soon, though, they moved the junior college off the university's premises altogether, to an old high school building in Joliet, forty miles to the south. In 1901, Joliet Junior College became the first community college in the nation. Soon afterward, junior colleges were founded in California, Missouri, and Michigan. Like those that followed, Joliet Junior College provided two years of general liberal arts education. The model wasn't preparing students for university, and it wasn't exactly preparing them for careers either. But it was providing access to postsecondary education for a wider variety of students than elite universities accommodated—a mission that endures today.

Within a decade, progressive policies were taking hold across the country, and higher education was expanding beyond a few elites. But all the Chicago-area colleges were private: the University of Chicago, the Armour Institute of Technology, Lewis Institute, DePaul, Loyola, and Northwestern. The nearest public university was more than one hundred miles away, in Champaign, Illinois. In an attempt to bring free public higher education to the city, in 1911 the Chicago Board of Education enrolled thirty-two boys in college credit courses at Crane Technical High School and Lane Technical School. The plan wasn't exactly well thought out—Crane teachers were told of the creation of "Crane Junior College" the day before classes started. And it was a very modest effort, serving only 0.0001 percent of the secondary system's 300,000 students.[3]

Within a decade, with the junior college receiving the support of both Democratic and Republican mayors, enrollment grew to a few thousand students—only 10 percent of eligible applicants—but limited finances prevented the construction of dedicated college campuses and expanded enrollment. The challenge of funding free college during the Great Depression became too much for Chicago, and the Board of Education closed Crane in 1933. But the same financial crisis that forced the closing of Crane also made reopening it imperative, for the students' sake. In 1934, the college was reopened, this time with dedicated funding, facilities, a curriculum designed by Crane staff and university faculty, and a new name: Chicago City Junior College. By the 1930s, in the throes of the Depression, community colleges nationwide had embraced job training as part of their mission. Chicago City Junior College, for example, adopted three major areas of emphasis: general education (required of all students), pre-professional training designed to prepare students to complete work at a four-year institution, and "terminal" semiprofessional training that would lead to jobs straight from junior college. At least in theory, the institution that would one day be renamed City Colleges of Chicago truly did have something for everybody.

This approach was reaffirmed after World War II, when the newly growing US consumer industry created a huge number of skilled jobs, and a massive influx of returning servicemen and women took advantage of the new GI Bill and enrolled in both senior and junior colleges. President Harry S Truman, after whom one of the City Colleges of Chicago would be named, appointed a commission to ensure that junior colleges would be able to handle the crush. In its final report, the commission rejected the belief that higher education "should be confined to an intellectual elite" but at the same time bought into the prevailing view that university was not for everyone. It embraced expanding the two-year model to stress "semiprofessional" training for jobs that did not require a four-year degree, which were actually more plentiful at the time. The report stressed, however, that these colleges "must not be crowded with vocational and technical courses to the exclusion of general education courses, but must instead aim at developing a combination of social understanding and technical competence."

The commission recommended replacing the term *junior college* with *community college*, because of the local nature of these institutions, and because their main focus would no longer be preparation for "senior" institutions.[4]

The community college sector would debate the term for decades. Did the name *community* mean, as many people continue to think, that a local college is supposed to serve only the community in its immediate vicinity, or was it meant to serve the global community or region (which is the right answer)? The debate can seem trivial, but the answer to the question can determine whether a community college can live up to its mission.

● ● ●

In 2009, the same year Mayor Daley approached me about the City Colleges job, momentum was building for a definition of college success that centered on degree completion, not just access. As noted in chapter 1, under President Obama's leadership, the federal government was taking steps to ask more of colleges: to prove that their students were graduating and attaining gainful employment. In July, Obama unveiled the American Graduation Initiative, which set a goal of 5 million additional college graduates by 2020 and centered on a proposed $12 billion revitalization of US community colleges. The initiative, Obama announced, "will reform and strengthen community colleges from coast to coast so that they get the resources students and schools need—and the results workers and businesses demand." Rarely had anyone publicly addressed the sector's worrisome track record, but the White House did. A statement accompanying the president's announcement elaborated: "Nearly half of students who enter community college intending to earn a degree or transfer to a four-year college fail to reach their goal within six years."[5] For the first time, the issue of community college outcomes was put at the heart of a national conversation that emanated from the Oval Office.

The initiative came on the heels of a few significant, eye-opening studies. In July, the President's Council of Economic Advisors published a report concluding that the demand for associate degrees was about to outpace the demand for bachelor's degrees. To truly serve students as well as the economy, the panel concluded, curricula had to be better aligned to employers' needs, and high remediation and dropout rates at community colleges had to be addressed.[6]

The same year, the Lumina Foundation, which focuses on postsecondary education, issued a report that set a goal of increasing the share of Americans with high-quality degrees and credentials from 39 percent to 60 percent by the year 2025.[7] In Illinois, the percent of working-age adults with at least a two-year degree was 36 percent, and in Chicago's Cook County, it was 42 percent. Illinois, the report found, had a huge opportunity to create more college graduates: 23 percent of the state's working-age population, or nearly 1.5 million people, had some college education, but no degree.

Bringing those folks back to complete what they started, Lumina argued, could provide a quick boost to both them and to businesses.[8]

In June 2010, just after I started at City Colleges, Professor Anthony Carnevale and his colleagues at Georgetown University's Center on Education and the Workforce published a report called *Help Wanted*, which came to some arresting conclusions. According to the report, by 2018 the United States would fall 3 million degrees and nearly 5 million certificates short of its workforce needs. The demands of employers had changed over time. In 1970, three-quarters of middle-class workers had no more than a high school degree; by 2007, only 40 percent did. One-third of middle-class workers had some college or an associate's degree, up from 12 percent four decades before. Americans who held associate degrees could expect nearly $500,000 more in lifetime earnings than those who only graduated high school.[9]

At the time, only a very few colleges were attempting whole-school reform. Many were implementing discrete programmatic reforms; for example, changing the way they delivered remedial instruction or requiring students to take study skills courses. A 2011 evaluation of Achieving the Dream, a national network of community colleges seeking to improve student outcomes, found that despite lots of effort, the reforms being implemented were benefiting only relatively small numbers of students and focused mainly on remediation and advising and not on the colleges' core academic programs.[10] At least the Achieving the Dream colleges were trying new approaches. Too many were doing nothing new at all.

Even where there was the will, there was no off-the-shelf model for transforming a large community college system into one that was single-mindedly focused on student outcomes. I believed that to create a whole-system reform that made the most sense for City Colleges and that would endure, we had to try to build it ourselves.

● ● ●

In the summer of 2010, three months into my tenure, I gathered the same group of leaders who had first flagged City Colleges' underperformance for Mayor Daley. Brian Fabes reminded everyone of the stakes: "Few students ever leave with a credential, and those who do find they can do very little with it."

When I started as chancellor, 45 percent of City College's students were pursuing a two-year associate degree, 6 percent were pursuing workforce certificates, 32 percent were enrolled in adult education, and 17 percent were taking classes for enrichment but not a credential. As far as we could tell, none of these groups were getting all that they came for.

The first step toward reform at City Colleges was identifying what, exactly, improvement would look like. What did student success mean, and what specific goals could we set to achieve it? Among us, we had the collective wisdom of decades of experience in education, business, and civic affairs. Those of us from the corporate world were familiar with the imperative of setting goals and measuring progress toward them. To define those goals was another matter—one that we couldn't do on our own. Fortunately, we had on our team one of the most respected figures in community college research and policy—Davis Jenkins, a Chicago resident and research scholar at Columbia University's Community College Research Center, had for many years been sounding the call for a success agenda, and helping states and colleges conceive and execute reforms. He ensured that our agenda for City Colleges would be grounded in a deep understanding of the field.

By the second day of our convening, with Jenkins' help we had settled on four academic goals, the core of the reform effort that we would eventually name "Reinvention":

1. *Increase the rate at which students complete college credentials of economic value to Chicago economy and communities.* This would be achieved by reducing barriers to completion and better aligning programs to employer and university requirements.
2. *Increase the rate and efficiency with which students transfer to bachelor's degree programs following graduation from City Colleges.* Most students were left to navigate the complex transfer process on their own, with the result that many quit in frustration or transferred with credits that were not accepted toward a bachelor's degree in their major field of interest. This goal required dramatic improvements in student supports, including advising and transfer support.

3. *Drastically improve outcomes for students requiring remediation.* Accomplishing this would require us to strengthen our partnership with Chicago Public Schools (to minimize the need for remediation in the first place) and to examine best practices nationwide to more quickly move students to credit-bearing courses.

4. *Increase the number and share of adult education, GED, and ESL students who advance to and succeed in college-level courses.* For this goal, we would need not only to help students meet their short-term goals of getting a GED or learning English as a second language, but also set the expectation for transitioning into college credit programs by building bridges to those programs, so students could meet goals they didn't even know they had yet.

Our leadership team supplemented these academic goals with goals for our operational effectiveness.

1. *Improve the quality and effectiveness of student services and support.* From admissions and advising through transfer and career placement, we had to provide effective supports to our students and remove barriers to success to encourage persistence and achievement. For efficiency, we had to move away from manual processes and invest more in information technology.

2. *Increase access to City Colleges, as measured by enrollment in programs that put students on the path to earning credentials of economic value.* While many of our goals were about student success, we also knew we needed to enroll more students in relevant programs to give them a better chance to complete—and compete—and also to make efficient use of our facilities and generate tuition revenue to ensure our financial well-being. We called this "enrollment with a purpose."

3. *Promote and reward effective teaching.* We knew we had to improve teaching quality and professional development; for example, by reforming the tenure process.

4. *Improve operational discipline with a focus on high performance standards, including excellent financial management.* We had to return money to the classroom by introducing best-practice operational efficiency to reduce non-instructional expenditures. Put plainly, we had to start operating with the rigor, restraint, and financial accountability of

a business. We needed to strengthen existing weak systems for financial management, external fundraising, and human resources management. Also, making the right strategic capital investments while
growing and maintaining our cash reserves would ensure that our facilities were suited to programs that provided the quality of preparation
our students needed to thrive in the workplace and further education.

5. *Ensure safe and secure teaching and learning environments.* The
safety and security of City Colleges students, faculty, and staff were
critical. We needed to make progress toward systematizing our security
best practices across all colleges to reduce crime on campus.

From now on, every existing and proposed program and student service, and every expenditure, would be evaluated using one simple question: *How does this advance our goals?*

City Colleges comprised seven colleges spread across the city. Each
was governed by its own president, set its own policies, and managed its
own budget. This in itself wasn't a problem; what had become a challenge was there was no common set of institutional goals. As it turns out,
it wasn't just the content of the system's goals that would turn out to be
wildly controversial—it was the idea of having clear strategic goals at all.

Everything I was learning about the community college sector nationally confirmed my instinct that this was the direction in which we needed
to head. For instance, that October, I joined about 150 experts from across
the country, as well as President Obama and Jill Biden, the Second Lady
and a community college educator, for the White House Summit on Community Colleges. Addressing us in front of the gilded drapery of the East
Room, Obama repeated his goal of making America once again the world
leader in the number of college graduates. He emphasized the main aim
of his American Graduation Initiative: "It's going to promote reform, as
colleges compete for funding by improving graduation rates, and matching courses to the needs of local businesses, and making sure that when
a graduate is handed a diploma, it means that she or he is ready for a
career." Administration officials and other experts articulated the value of
granting more credentials, tracking progress through metrics, providing
students with better guidance, coordinating with four-year institutions to

boost transfer, and creating meaningful partnerships with employers so that students were gaining the right skills and knowledge.[11]

Attending this event was a huge honor and thrill. As I walked up to the gate of the White House, I could not help but think about how far I had come from the Henry Horner Homes. And I knew my parents were bursting with pride back home. (My late grandmother would have been too.) But even more gratifying was hearing everyone at the White House speaking a language similar to how we talked about Reinvention. Now I just had to get people used to this language—and passionate about it—back home. For those who were still resistant to our vision, the work would be full-on threatening. Even for those who were beginning to get on board with this vision, change was going to be difficult. This was a journey that few at City Colleges of Chicago—or any US community colleges—had ever attempted as aggressively as we were about to, and there weren't maps to guide us.

Reinvention put us on the front lines of a nascent nationwide effort to bring relevance back to community colleges. The model is based on a simple principle that drives private-sector enterprises and many in the public sector as well, but from which some parts of higher education frustratingly seem exempt: *Organizations must be accountable for providing results.* This should be especially true for organizations funded by taxpayers. My insistence on this provoked a resistance that would ultimately become very personal. But in the meantime, we set out to create those results.

• • •

Our early internal consultations made it clear that for our reform efforts to succeed, we needed more than goals. We needed a common understanding of what was ailing us and our students. We needed to make the case for change.

This isn't unique to City Colleges, or to the education sector, for that matter. Any major institutional reform depends on stakeholders—in this case, faculty, administrators, and staff—sharing the conviction that change is urgently needed. We needed to communicate not just an understanding of the problem but a clearly articulated reason for change, centered around our mission.

So at the beginning of October 2010, my new leadership team and I embarked on a series of town hall meetings across the colleges. Through a PowerPoint presentation we called "The Case for Change," we explained the need and vision for Reinvention. We stressed that City Colleges always had been a beacon of hope, and the institution as it stood was well positioned but poorly organized to help students succeed and help Chicago remain competitive.

First, we painstakingly documented the myriad ways City Colleges had been falling short, through a number of important data points:

- While jobs requiring credentials provided by community colleges were growing, City Colleges enrollment had declined 30 percent from 1998 to 2008.
- Only 7 percent of first-time, full-time students who came to City Colleges for a credential earned it within 150 percent of the program time; for instance, within three years for a two-year associate degree.
- Fifty-four percent of degree-seeking students dropped out within their first six months.
- More than 90 percent of incoming students needed remediation.
- About 80 percent of programs graduated fewer than forty students per entering class, and many of these programs were out of step with industry demand.
- Only 35 percent of adult education met their stated goal—for instance, to earn a GED—each year.

We highlighted not just the fact that too few students (both degree-seeking and adult education) were leaving without a credential, but also the reality that a credential did not ensure that a graduate had learned the skills necessary to compete in today's society. Simply put, we were not transforming students' lives at scale.

Next, we laid out our vision for the fix: Reinvention would be a bottom-up effort in which everyone would have a voice in determining the remedies. The idea was that administrators, who made the initial Case for Change by analyzing internal and national data and best practices, would write the next chapters together with students, faculty, staff, and external stakeholders.

To underscore the depth of our problems, our presentation compared City Colleges with other institutions (see figure 2.1). Among the forty-nine

FIGURE 2.1

2010 comparison of City Colleges to other community colleges

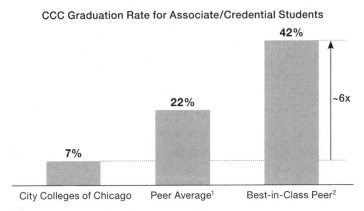

CCC Graduation Rate for Associate/Credential Students

[1]Based on 2006 IPEDS national benchmarks vs. peers of similar size, degree/certificate offerings. Includes urban and suburban institutions. Allowed for 150% of recommended time to completion.

[2]90th percentile institution in IPEDS graduation rate.

Source: Fall 2005 entering cohort reported to IPEDS; team analysis.

community colleges in Illinois, all of ours were in the bottom nine in terms of graduation rate. Our 7 percent rate was less than one-third the average for our peer group—institutions of a size similar to our individual colleges that primarily awarded certificates and associate degrees and had a significantly non-white student body.[12]

Our leadership changes did not end with me. Despite the admonishments of some of my advisers, who thought the disruption to the system would be too great, but with the encouragement and support of others, I decided to conduct a search for new college presidents and to require six of the seven current presidents, all of whom had come up the ranks conventionally through City Colleges, to reapply for their job—if they wanted to. The seventh president had already resigned, and we replaced him with a business executive who had experience in higher education. We wrote a new job description that highlighted the four goals of Reinvention, as well as the presidents' accountability for meeting them (this included rewriting my job description as well). We wanted to ensure that we had the best possible leaders in place, and that they were committed to the hard work of reform. Several would reapply, but I kept only one.

Even though the new presidents also had a higher education background, the backlash was fierce. Some media, community groups, elected officials, students, and faculty lashed out. My speaking about the need for reform was one thing, but replacing nearly all the presidents? Changing leadership to address poor outcomes is widely accepted—even demanded— in business. But in academia, at least at City Colleges, this loud signal that the status quo was about to be overturned came as an unwelcome shock.

We had been hearing repeatedly from some faculty, staff, and external stakeholders that there weren't any problems to fix. In most instances, I believe that people found it inherently difficult to acknowledge and accept the problems because they were afraid of the institution being perceived as a failure. Some may have been afraid of the accountability that came with that, and some may have taken it as a personal attack. I, however, was trying as best I could to present these issues as an opportunity to become a national model for reform because I knew that low expectations and accepting the status quo could ultimately defeat the will to do better. A few months after I took office, an anonymous writer published a blog that repeatedly took issue with "the Chancellor's invalid claim that the community colleges of Chicago are failing."[13] For every weakness we raised, someone had a response: The graduation rate wasn't a good measure because it didn't grant students enough time, or it failed to count part-time students. Or it didn't properly account for students who attended City Colleges without the goal of a credential, such as those who transferred and completed their bachelor's elsewhere without having earned an associate degree. The simple fact of whether or not a student completed a credential, detractors said, didn't capture the full breadth of the college's contributions to his or her life. "Our students struggle more than other colleges' students," they argued, "so we shouldn't compare ourselves to them."

People satisfied with the status quo at City Colleges also pointed to a longitudinal study completed in 2008, which had found a combined transfer/degree completion rate of 29 percent over six years—much higher than the 7 percent (over three years) that we were stressing.[14] Of the 17 percent of students who transferred to a four-year institution, fewer than 5 percent graduated with a bachelor's degree, while 64 percent of the students studied demonstrated achievement in *one* of several criteria. But my leadership team and I were underwhelmed by what the study treated as evidence of success. One criterion was achieving a C average—which meant a student likely had D's or F's balancing out some higher grades. Another criterion was that students stayed enrolled from year to year—necessary, of course, but not sufficient. Even the fact that students were transferring didn't necessarily indicate progress, since just as many transferred to another community college as did to a four-year institution. That students left City Colleges for other area community or for-profit colleges hardly validated our quality.

Our presentations proactively addressed these arguments. Yes, the graduation rate didn't count part-time students, but reworking the formula to do so would only add 1 percentage point. If we calculated the graduation rate giving students six years to complete, rather than the three we used (a standard measure), the completion rate would increase to 13 percent, but we would still lag well behind our peers—and anyway, accepting that students should take six years to complete a two-year degree did them a disservice. Crediting students who get bachelor's but no associate degrees would not have changed the equation much, because very few students did this.

And the idea that our students were somehow different than those at other colleges? Certainly, growing up in poverty amid the violence of Chicago is a heavy burden—I knew this as well as anyone. Working and raising kids while going to school is an extreme challenge too. But such is the reality for community college students across the nation, one-third of whom have family incomes below $20,000, two-thirds of whom work while in college, and 30 percent of whom are parents.[15] While it was our responsibility to do far better by these students—for instance, through advising, course scheduling, tutoring, and other support services—it was unthinkable to me that we would assume they couldn't be successful.

The point was this: whatever the measure, whatever the criteria, whatever the formula, City Colleges was punching way below its weight, and thus was not serving the students and the city to the extent that it could and it should. We needed to resist the temptation to use our students' struggles as excuses for our own failures. Other institutions were doing far better with similar students. Rather than assume that our students needed to be more college-ready, our responsibility was to ensure that our colleges were much more student-ready.

Our aim in laying out the data was not to put people down; it was meant as a wake-up call for action based on the premise that we all had gotten into this line of work to help students help themselves through education. We made sure that the Case for Change highlighted pockets of excellence throughout the system: radiography students passing their national registry exam at a rate higher than the national average, a bilingual program with a high completion rate, a dental hygiene program with a 100 percent pass rate on the national board exam, a nephrology and renal technology program where nearly every graduate got a job.[16]

Surely, I'd thought, once stakeholders saw the dismal success numbers, they would be on board. I knew that some leaders at some institutions, including community colleges, managed to marshal support for reform simply by laying out data showing poor outcomes. And at first, the comments and questions I got were for the most part polite and curious. Several faculty and staff told me how happy they were to see an African American, female former student come back as chancellor. The leadership team and I were mainly met with what seemed like indifference. Most faculty and staff did not react on way or another. That was fine with me—this was a lot to process! Many said they would keep an open mind because higher outcomes would always be good.

For some faculty, however, the Case for Change, intended as a wakeup call, served instead as a rallying cry for opposition—a dubious justification, they said, for a corporate takeover of the community college system that would profit big companies while cutting investment in professional development.

I wasn't totally unprepared for opposition. In fact, at our very first meeting in the Reinvention road show, I could tell that I was coming across as too negative. My personality is that I want people to tell me things as they are, and my experience in business was that blunt assessments were the norm. So I reworked the presentation, softening my approach. But it turned out to not be that simple. Even the reworked presentation, the one I had *softened*, felt like a punch in the gut to some of these people who had dedicated their lives to helping students, rather than focusing on improving the low performance.

And I didn't fully anticipate that the Case for Change would be felt as a personal attack. Or that detractors would soon be launching personal and offensive attacks against me. For example, an anonymous blog devoted to City Colleges issues derided my "West Side" of Chicago diction and syntax in addition to my business background. "They cherry picked the data and then used it to provide an excuse for transforming a system that, as all the data show, didn't need to be transformed," someone later wrote. The presentation was dismissed as "market speak"; my insistence there was a problem despite the 2008 data showed I was "delusional." Instead of pointing out where City Colleges was falling short, one blogger wrote, I should "use positive organizational psychology to 'sell' the institution by using 'real' data to encourage productivity."[17]

But although I was shocked, I had a thick skin about the attacks—they wouldn't stand in the way of improvement. Reluctance to acknowledge a problem, however, could.

● ● ●

Taken together, this resistance reflected one of the greatest barriers to community college improvement, at City Colleges and throughout the sector. Many in academia and civil society are still coming to grips with the full extent of the problems facing the national resource that is the community college. As more and more educators, community leaders, and government officials attempt to bring about a tectonic cultural and operational shift to more fully connect community colleges to the expectations of those who enroll in them and those who rely on their graduates, they face this disconnect, whether it takes the form of blog posts or votes of no confidence or simply a refusal to change. The disconnect is not the result of ill will, but of a decades-old culture that failed to emphasize relevance, accountability, and data.

And, of course, there was the insularity of academia. Even when I managed to convince people there was a problem, they could not accept that "outsiders" like me could solve it.

CHAPTER 3

THE BUSINESS OF REINVENTION

New Principles and Processes

In 2008, I was a lobbyist for Commonwealth Edison—improving outcomes and efficiency was not my job. But I suggested to our CEO that we needed an internal strategy team that would work with leaders across ComEd's business units to identify obstacles to efficiency and growth, and work with his leadership team on possible solutions. The goal couldn't just be cost-cutting by eliminating line items, because you simply cannot cut your way to being a good company. Rather, we needed to focus on efficiency and better allocation of our time and assets. The strategy team would gather input, study trends and best practices across the energy sector and beyond, analyze internal data, and recommend processes and procedures to drive long-term efficiency and improve productivity for the company.

A few weeks later, the CEO told me that he had thought it over. It was a good idea, he said, and he wanted me to help manage the new team. A couple of weeks later, thrilled but also scared that I had to make good on my own idea, I was officially reassigned as co-lead for the effort. The stakes were high, because ComEd's financial operating results—cost and revenue—were headed in the wrong direction. Our mission was to conceive, evaluate, and implement high-impact strategies to help drive revenue and bring down operating costs.

Our team had three parts: a research team to monitor progress and identify external trends and best practices; a strategic initiatives group to analyze operations and recommend changes; and an operational analysis team to evaluate the strategic team's recommendations and monitor anything we implemented. This was management consulting of sorts, but from within, as the teams would be made up of a diverse set of employees from different parts of the company who would step away from their day jobs and devote months, full-time, to this effort.

Within two years, the company, through this initiative as well as efforts by ComEd's operations, customer service, and governmental affairs teams, had significantly curbed operating and maintenance costs and identified new sources of revenue. The initiative was highlighted in the company's annual report as contributing to the company's overall success, with results in part derived from "delivering on the commitment of continuous improvement and performance optimization." The internal consulting arm still exists today and, by identifying potential efficiencies and promoting best practices, has saved the company millions and generated a significant amount of revenue.

While my work was only part of the companywide move toward efficiency, I took great pride in the outcome, and learned the power of data-driven management and collaborative strategy development, due in large part to the incredibly smart team I was so fortunate to have. Perhaps the best capstone to the company's fifteen-year effort and my small role in it was that in July 2011, Chicago experienced one of the worst heat waves since 1995, and ComEd was able to meet the high demand for power.

The ComEd and Exelon (its parent company) executives had executed what I consider a textbook turnaround, and I'd take more than a page from this book as chancellor of City Colleges.

• • •

If there's one thing educators don't like to hear, it's that education should be run more like a business. But that's something that needs to be said and acted on much more. It's true that public colleges are unlike companies in that they don't have a profit motive. But in their obligation to demand efficiency and accountability, to maximize the potential of limited resources, and to effectively serve their customers—the students—colleges must pursue sound finances and management practices.

What did it mean that I was going to run City Colleges like a business? We would create a set of specific, clearly defined outcome targets and hold people accountable for meeting them. Any change would be assessed through an analytic, data-centered process—one that still factored in experience and judgment but became more evidence-based. We would cut costs by operating more efficient where we could to redirect money toward student success and pursue what evidence determined our students needed, not what everyone else preferred. Running City Colleges like a business also meant, unfortunately, that I would quickly get on the wrong side of some professors and community groups who could not abide the idea of this way of operating, no matter what the actual changes were.

I went into the effort with five key assumptions, derived from my corporate experience and cemented by my early experiences at City Colleges:

- *Culture:* We needed to focus explicitly on defining, building, and sustaining cultural change centered on student success, which meant transforming mindsets, capabilities, and behaviors for all employee groups. More than a set of initiatives, Reinvention had to be a mindset where we were not afraid to face reality and change and discard sacred cows.
- *Accountability:* It is vital to be clear-eyed about academic and operational performance, so that improvement opportunities can be charted. We had to develop a detailed management structure and performance metrics by which to evaluate success.
- *Planning:* We had to define and map specific changes to directly improve and sustain performance, all articulated in a multiyear plan that set numerical objectives for operations and academic improvement.
- *Collaboration:* Internal collaboration and external consultation would be a prerequisite for a smart improvement process.
- *Training:* Strategic initiatives had to be accompanied by information and training, so administrators and faculty would understand the rationale and potential of new approaches and master the best techniques to implement them.

I spent my first hundred days as chancellor looking at a mass of data—from past internal reports, information submitted to the state and federal authorities, and more—to assess the colleges' results. From every data point flowed a number of questions: How long did it take students to get a GED, and what happened to them after they did? How many students attended only until shortly after they got their financial aid disbursement, and why did they leave so soon? I called person after person into my office, and couldn't get a satisfactory answer.

As at many community colleges, the institutional research department was used to responding to requests for reports and synthesizing information, but didn't proactively seek to obtain, analyze, and organize data or act on it. I knew we needed a new approach. I hired a vice chancellor of strategy and institutional intelligence as my chief strategist—Alvin Bisarya, an MD from Northwestern who spent five years as an engagement manager for McKinsey Consulting in addition to being a former high school biology teacher—to dig through the data and organize our approach to and recommendations for improvements against the four reinvention goals (see chapter 2). Eventually, this team developed into a full-fledged strategy department under Rasmus Lynnerup (who later replaced Alvin), who would oversee three units designed to proactively conduct research and operational analyses and implement strategic initiatives through internal consulting teams that would be a cornerstone of my strategy. We even built a new physical space so that everyone involved in this effort could work side by side.

Our work would be divided into four phases (see figure 3.1). Phase 1—defining our institutional goals—had already happened. During winter 2010 and spring 2011, phase 2 would be devoted to collaborative problem solving, where rotating task forces of faculty, students, and staff would make recommendations as to the main priorities identified in phase 1. During phase 3, administrators would join forces with task force members to implement the recommendations. Then, I had envisioned, we'd move into phase 4, where we would work to make change sustainable by institutionalizing best practices and setting up a culture where consultation and continual improvement would be part of our everyday lives.

• • •

FIGURE 3.1

The phases of Reinvention, as articulated in 2010

Initial diagnostic	Develop recommendations via task forces	Implement recommendations across seven colleges	Sustain and renew system-wide change
July–Dec 2010	*Jan–May 2011*	*June 2011–June 2012*	*June 2012 and beyond*
Identify high-level priorities	Conduct deeper dive into priority areas	Implement priority recommendations for scalable solutions from task force efforts	Scaled, sustainable, effective, and segmented solutions are permanent and sigificantly improving student success across all City Colleges
Design, staff, and launch task forces	Continue to develop, plan, and prioritize recommendations	Refine/enhance recommendations throughout the implementation process	New task force teams will return each semester
Design and assemble advisory committees	Identify and begin pursuing quick wins	Continue to measure CCC performance; compare expected task force impact versus actual results	
	Engage broader community		

Throughout

Student-focused—orienting all solutions to what will be of most benefit to current and future students

Data-driven—measuring results, reflecting on what is/isn't working and working to improve

Even at the best-intentioned community colleges, reform often simply consists of an agglomeration of new programmatic strategies. But as with any institution, colleges cannot be truly transformed without a more profound shift of culture and focus. It's not just about adding programs. You have to create the right conditions for the new programs to work. You have to have a clear vision that drives the creation and adoption of the strategies, a consistent process to analyze which ones you need and whether they work, and personnel practices and policies that ensure that the right people have the right tools to do the work. If I could give one thing to City Colleges during my tenure, it was a structure that would enable the institution—and others that might look to us as a model—to always make the best choices for student success while keeping operations efficient.

Both practically and culturally, my approach was a huge change for City Colleges. For too long, as at many community colleges, enrollment was the main indicator of success. The strategic plan in progress when I arrived centered on inputs, not outcomes. The closest it came to a focus on student success was to say, "We welcome students—wherever they are—and assist them in achieving their educational goals and full potential."[1] To build a better reputation for City Colleges among local stakeholders, this plan suggested improving public appreciation through marketing—not by producing better graduates. Its twenty-four pages touted dynamic curriculum, diversity, globalization, and student learning outcomes, but there was not one mention of degree completion.

Given our new direction and goals, I thought we needed new leadership as well—people who brought both academic and business expertise. This proved controversial; many people inside colleges believe that administrators should always come up through the academic ranks. Certainly, for jobs focused on teaching and learning, a PhD is sometimes a vital credential, and many of those who drove our reforms and led our colleges throughout Reinvention held doctorates. But for overhauling the strategic and systemic operations of a $700 million organization, we needed a mix of people with directly relevant experience in areas like change management, as well as a solid commitment to focus on outcomes and accountability.

I especially wanted to surround myself with people smarter than me, people who brought different life experiences, perspectives, and professional expertise. Given my strong personality, I also wanted to work with people who were not intimidated and were willing to challenge me.

I called several former utility colleagues, as well as former business school classmates. Some were deterred by politics or public-sector salaries. Others were daunted by City Colleges' reputation. All declined my offers, and just about all of them questioned my sanity in taking the job. So I asked my broader circle of business acquaintances whether they knew anyone who, like me, was willing to trade a high private-sector income for a chance to change lives.

A few brave souls raised their hands. Soon, we had added not only Alvin Bisarya as vice chancellor of strategy and institutional intelligence, but Ron Anderson, who had worked many years in the education sector, as chief of staff to act as an orchestra conductor (Ron would later be replaced by Craig Lynch, who had previously been our vice chancellor of information technology). I also hired Jim Frankenbach, who was highly respected in the healthcare industry and the former CEO of a hospital as a consultant for our health care programs; he would later become our full-time chief operating officer to make sure we accounted for every dollar, maximized operational efficiency, and redirected as much of our funds as possible to advancing student success. While Ron came from education, Jim and Alvin had private-sector backgrounds. As we started out, we also worked with a consulting firm (at an extreme discount) and engaged with the Civic Consulting Alliance to help advise us and access external data.

The new leadership team's lack of higher education experience, the involvement of civic and business leaders in our efforts, and the fact that we were adding a new layer of staff to the payroll to take on a new set of responsibilities aroused anger from some inside as well as outside of City Colleges. What we saw as a necessary step to improve efficiency and improve student outcomes, our critics saw as an example of bloated bureaucracy and the incursion of outsiders: administrators only sucked up money that would be better spent otherwise. This assumption was not unique to City Colleges, because I hear it everywhere I go: administrators are just overhead who don't offer much value to educational institutions. I couldn't disagree more. We were about to improve student outcomes in a way City Colleges had never seen before, and there was no way we could have accomplished that without our talented and passionate administrators. Furthermore, we were about to cut, not increase, the money we spent on administration overall and redirect it to the classroom. By the end of my tenure, City Colleges would save $70 million by decreasing inefficiencies and would reduce spending on administrative overhead by 6 percent. Spending on activities related to the core academic mission, like instruction and student services, would increase 9 percent.

There was also an irony in this critique of new administrators: the new system we were building would depend on meaningful engagement, innovation, and problem solving by faculty, staff, and students. But the outsiders who had just become leaders of this institution might be the first to truly listen.

• • •

A few weeks into Reinvention, Alvin Bisarya was leading a brainstorm with faculty members about solving one of the most vexing problems in US higher education: remediation. He had called this meeting to collect best practices and ideas on moving forward. Instead, he found himself quickly engaged in a tense debate, which was rooted in two main issues. One was a general attitude that remediation was a problem that was caused by, and thus could only be solved by, the K–12 system. The other was conviction on the part of some faculty members that a team led by non-academics could never understand the needs of students and the plight of teachers, much less devise solutions. In particular, a tenured science professor argued that neither City Colleges nor any other community college in the country had been able to fix the remediation problem. Who was "District Office" to think that it could? The professor viewed Reinvention as a top-down effort like those that had come before, where edicts were handed down without faculty input.

After several minutes of back-and-forth, Alvin pivoted. "This is not just about what I think," he said. "What do *you* think we should do?" The professor seemed taken aback. After a moment of reflection, he said, "Nobody from District Office has ever asked me that."

This faculty member wasn't alone in his wariness of me and my team. From the earliest hour, there was forceful and at times hostile disagreement by some City College employees with what we were doing. But his response demonstrated a key part of our strategy: to use our taskforce model as a way to try and turn detractors into involved contributors

Around that same time, I met with leaders of the Faculty Council, (a group of thirty employees selected by full-time faculty members from across City Colleges district) who had questions about the Case for Change and the direction Reinvention was taking. Their concerns were over shared governance—that the centralization of some decisions and processes would infringe on academic freedom. I reminded them that none of our initiatives had stepped, or would step, into the classroom or between students and their teachers. I laid out my vision of our respective roles. I would leave academic issues to faculty but that although they would still have input about administration, support systems, processes, and budgets, these were areas that could benefit from a more disciplined approach managed by administrators. That struck me as the main issue with the definition of shared governance: It felt they wanted the say in governance without the accountability that should come with it. Nobody could tell me who was supposed to share what with whom. I just knew in the end, I would be held accountable for it all.

Yet from the beginning, I had been committed to consultation with students, faculty, and staff. For instance, when we hired new college presidents, with the exception of a few cases where we had to act quickly, committees of faculty, staff, administrators, and students interviewed the presidential candidates and gave me recommendations. Many leaders think this kind of engagement is a good way to increase stakeholders' "buy-in" to reform and ensure its implementation. I suppose that is true. But more important, we needed them to *create* the reform. They knew better than anyone the obstacles to change and possible ways to overcome them. While some may have been in the dark about the low level of achievement, and while there may have been disagreements over the scope of and reasons for the problems, most people who came to work at City Colleges, especially faculty, had chosen their job to help students. They believed that education was a force to improve society. And they were the ones doing the hard work in classrooms and offices every day.

There was another key factor at play. When I became chancellor, there was new national impetus for community college reform centered on student success, but no playbook. President Obama's 2009 call for community college reform would spawn a lot of research and investment into this issue by both government and foundations, and several books and reports would eventually map out promising solutions, but at the time we didn't have many outside resources.[2]

Certainly there was plenty of interest from foundations to fund initiatives. Foundations can be tremendously helpful in supporting short-term, time-bound, discrete efforts. They also have the resources to influence more of the outcomes we need to see in higher education, and we were thankful for the support we received.

But I have several fundamental beliefs when it comes to seeking external assistance. First, though it's a massive challenge, organizations that are attempting large-scale systemic change for the first time may benefit from building the process themselves. This allows them to own the change. Those involved in the effort take pride in their involvement and end up serving as ambassadors for change, thus improving chances of widespread buy-in. I also believe strongly that before any organization seeks external financial help, it should clean its own house—ensure it is operating efficiently, have a strategic plan in which external partners can invest, and be able to clearly articulate what the return on investment will be for the investor. Finally, at most organizations, and certainly at City Colleges, there was enough experience and intelligence internally to define workable models. For these reasons, I didn't want an externally designed blueprint or an embedded team of experts, which I thought would have only intensified the resistance.

We visited several community colleges known to already be achieving results from new reforms. At Valencia College in Orlando, Florida, one of the country's largest community colleges, the graduation rate was nearly three times that of other large, urban community colleges. Over a decade, Valencia had nearly tripled its graduation rate for college-ready African American students and increased the rate for college-ready Hispanic students by 17 percent. (The "college-ready" part is of course a big caveat, but nonetheless this was a very significant indicator of improvement.) Led by President Sanford Shugart, Valencia had launched, among other initiatives, a strong transfer partnership with nearby University of Central Florida and a wraparound support and advising model called LifeMap, which helped students chart their path to a career and provided the help they needed along the way.[3] At Valencia, we noticed, change was being embraced by faculty, students, and staff even if everyone didn't always agree on every aspect of reform.

At City Colleges, it appeared, few administrators and faculty had ever been presented with data about institutional performance and student outcomes, much less asked to think through and propose solutions that went beyond their own classroom or department to drive change on an institutional scale. But that was about to change.

● ● ●

In October 2010, we sent an invitation for all City Colleges students and employees to join Reinvention task forces, teams that would study important issue areas and make recommendations for reform (see figure 3.2).

(Initially, there were task forces for seven topics and related priorities, but an eighth, capital planning, was added later as we became smarter about our program offerings.):

1. Program portfolio design:
   - Revamp program offerings to increase the economic value of credentials earned at City Colleges by aligning with the needs of the marketplace.
   - Increase the number of transfers by better understanding the requirements of four-year institutions.

FIGURE 3.2
The task force structure as illustrated in Reinvention: Chapter 1 in 2010

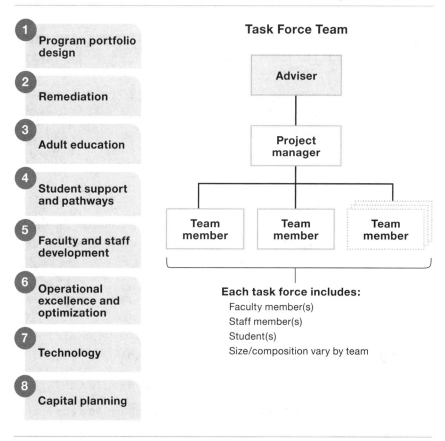

2. Remediation:
   - Drastically improve outcomes for students requiring remediation.
   - Develop approaches to more quickly move all students needing remediation into credit programs.
   - Partner with Chicago Public Schools and others.
3. Adult education:
   - Focus on increasing both the absolute number and proportion of adult basic education, GED, and ESL students who advance to and succeed in college-level courses.
4. Student support and pathways:
   - Improve advising, tutoring, job placement (in area of study), transfer support, and other supports.
   - Ensure each and every student has the best chance to succeed at City Colleges.
   - Ensure the institution provides an easy way to navigate the system and complete in a timely manner.
5. Faculty and staff development:
   - Improve the supports and developmental opportunities to enable faculty and staff to serve our students
6. Operational excellence and optimization:
   - Improve the return on investment of non-instructional funds invested across the colleges.
   - Build an investment strategy fully aligned to driving student success.
7. Technology:
   - Build the technological capabilities and systems to drive significant improvement in City Colleges' data integrity, instructional technology, and non-instructional/support technology.
8. Capital planning:
   - Develop a plan to address years of neglected maintenance that will reflect the latest changes in pedagogy and technology.
   - Develop a clear capital investment strategy for the future of City Colleges to ensure we have modernized facilities to prepare students for twenty-first-century careers

The topic task forces were charged with determining how the institution was doing and where it fell short in terms of the new goals, identifying pain points and root causes, gathering stakeholder feedback, studying what peers and best-in-class institutions were doing, and generating feasible, scalable solutions. The teams would have to develop business plans that laid out everything from potential costs of a solution (via economic modeling) to the workflow to a communications and change management plan for implementation. Knowing that every suggestion couldn't be implemented, my senior leadership team would choose from the recommendations, which were scored on criteria including potential impact on student success, student satisfaction, and operational improvement as well as costs. Once a solution was approved, the task forces would have to conduct workshops to engage the affected stakeholders and modify the plans based on their feedback.

In our haste, we had originally meant to launch the task forces midsemester. However, when faculty let us know that leaving their students midterm was a bad idea (of course!), we moved the start to January. The invitation memo implored faculty, staff, and students to consider serving:

> We were excited to see so many of you at the Case for Change presentation held at all seven colleges on Friday, October 1, 2010. Many people expressed a sincere desire to help in the effort to reinvent the City Colleges. It's going to take a real commitment from all of us to make this transformation a success. . . .
>
> Being a team member will not only be of great benefit to CCC and our students, it will also be an exciting challenge for you, one that promises to stretch and develop you professionally, expose you to new topics and techniques, and work hand in hand with District leadership to accomplish something truly transformational.

Each task force would be composed of eight to ten members—faculty, staff, senior administrators, and students—as well as an experienced project manager (staff members hired from both outside and inside City Colleges to work for the new strategy director and paid for through operational savings) and an adviser (a college president, vice president, or vice chancellor). While the eight original task forces would last throughout my tenure, participants would take part for at least one semester, then cycle out so that others could serve and so that they could return to their departments

as ambassadors and advocates, sharing what they had learned and proposed. The achievement of tenure aside, there is not a lot of upward mobility for faculty; the task forces would be a way to foster the development of
new skills for talented professionals and identify people for future leadership opportunities.

Faculty members and staff on the task forces were paid their salaries
but were completely relieved of their everyday duties. (The taskforce work
became their full-time job and they were relocated to the district office
where the taskforces worked everyday. The relief period varied depending
on the project, but it was never less than a complete semester and some
lasted a year or longer.) Students were paid, too, though their compensa-
tion was capped at twenty hours a week to preserve time for their academic
work. Those unable to commit the time required to be on a task force could
serve on ad hoc committees that would meet periodically with task forces,
volunteer to serve on focus groups, or simply submit ideas via email.

Each group had at least one student or employee from each of the
seven colleges. All community colleges seem to have silos that separate
departments and offices, and faculty and administrators. But at City Colleges, we also suffered from the divisions inherent in a system of seven
independently operated colleges. (The fact that they are called colleges, not
campuses, speaks to the degree they were operating as standalone institutions.) We hoped that the task forces would break down these divisions. I
understood that everyone was, and should have been, proud of their individual colleges, but they needed to understand and embrace the power of a
system. They also needed to understand that if one campus failed, it would
be viewed as a failure of the entire system.

Task force members were trained in facilitation and feasibility assessment and were given a four-step work cycle:

1. Define the problem.
2. Structure the approach.
3. Analyze.
4. Synthesize findings and develop recommendations.[4]

In response to concerns that the project managers and advisers might
be overly directive or muzzle the task force members, we trained the staff

on how to be effective moderators and facilitators, but knew it was something we would have to monitor very closely.

The task forces would not only draw on their own experiences, but would also consult with external advisory council experts in academia, business, community and civic organizations, and capital planning. The Academic Council was co-chaired by a former university administrator and a Chicago Public Schools Board member, the Business Council by the heads of the Chicagoland Chamber of Commerce and the Illinois Hispanic Chamber of Commerce, the Civic/Foundation Council by a Chicago philanthropist and a regional foundation executive, and the Community Advisory Council by the head of a prominent community-based organization and a consultant to social impact organizations.[5]

Three hundred students, faculty, and staff applied to be on a task force. Nearly seventy-five were initially selected, 45 percent of them faculty and 25 percent students. Starting in late 2010, team members consulted with the advisory councils, researched articles and case studies, conducted phone interviews, and even visited community colleges that had achieved strong outcomes, including Valencia Community College in Florida, City University of New York, Ivy Tech in Indiana, and Maricopa Community Colleges in Arizona.[6]

In addition to members' collaboration within task forces, it was important for the task forces to interact with each other. The new Reinvention floor of the district office housed institutional research, the task forces, and the permanent Reinvention staff. The chief strategist's office had glass walls covered in different people's handwriting—a visible symbol of how so many smart and dedicated people were coming together to generate brilliant ideas to help our students. I visited the floor almost daily.

As the task forces finished their work, the recommendations were compiled in a 250-page report, also synthesized in a roughly 65-page summary, both put online for everyone to read. The sum of the recommendations reflected a seminal collaborative effort and, though they would be refined, these recommendations were the genesis of just about every success that would emerge from Reinvention. The problems the eight task forces identified seem obvious in retrospect, but the solutions were not. In many cases they would require far-reaching operational changes and a significant reallocation of resources.

As we tackled this huge institutional reform project, it was important for us to not just understand what City Colleges needed to change, but whether we were approaching reform in an effective manner. We surveyed task force members at three points in the process to gauge whether they felt empowered to explore and make recommendations freely, whether the effort was worthwhile, and whether we needed to change how we managed the process. In February 2011, a few weeks into the task forces' work, 91 percent of respondents said they were excited about the work they were doing. On the question of being empowered and not receiving too much direction from task force leaders and advisers, 70 percent agreed, 18 percent were neutral, and 12 percent disagreed. Nearly nine in ten participants said they'd recommend serving on a task force to a colleague.[7] At the conclusion of the work, in late March, the numbers slid a bit, but the feedback remained overwhelmingly positive: 81 percent of respondents still agreed they were excited about participating on their task force, 69 percent felt empowered and felt that they did not receive too much direction, and 77 percent said they would recommend serving on a task force.[8]

It was a concern that 31 percent of participants felt the process was at times too controlled by the administration. A faculty blog conducted a qualitative survey of task force members' morale, and one respondent reflected this sentiment:

> We are under stress to get things done quickly, and we are working hard to make sure that quality is not overlooked in favor of expediency. Morale is high when we can all agree on a solution, and begin to move forward with it. Morale is low when we are road blocked either within our team, by advisors or by the district leadership. Morale is low when we are 'urged' to take on a task that the task force team has not bought into.[9]

Others were more upbeat. One faculty member wrote:

> [City Colleges] set the stage and we (the players) had the freedom to play our role on stage. We've had a great deal of liberty to determine our direction, our efforts and ultimately decisions for recommendations."[10]

A student member wrote,

It's important that students know their opinion counts . . . Your comments are reviewed and compiled into data. This is one way that Reinvention members can make recommendations about what is, or is not working on each campus . . . I was not treated as a student but equally as a task force member."[11]

Once the recommendations were complete, various staff members and task force members fanned across the system to present them to City Colleges employees. Alvin Bisarya led a nearly daylong event, attended by a few hundred people, with posters that synthesized each group's work and breakout sessions led by task force members. We wanted anyone who worked at City Colleges to have a chance to ask questions and weigh in. The sessions were well attended and collegial, and a sense of common purpose permeated the event.

Not all the feedback was positive. I hoped that skeptics would see how thorough the work was and keep an open mind, but right away, faculty members confronted Alvin with questions that presaged some difficulties ahead. They wanted to know if we would implement all the recommendations, if we would make any tweaks as we implemented them, and whether we intended to have all aspects of Reinvention decided in this collaborative manner in the future—likely a rhetorical question, as we had already said that we would be making some operational and academic changes. He responded that we would likely have to prioritize and adapt some of the recommendations for various operational, budgetary, and tactical reasons. Some of the more skeptical faculty members who had not been on task forces left the conversation feeling disenfranchised, convinced that this had all just been a show and that the district office would do whatever it wanted regardless of input or recommendations by faculty.

About the time the task forces were drafting their final reports, vocal opposition to Reinvention was bubbling up not just internally but externally. For example, a publication known for in-depth analysis of local issues published a feature titled "The 7 Percent Solution," which expressed skepticism about our "collaborative" task force process: "From the baseline that's been drawn," the article said about the graduation rate, "there's

nowhere to go but up. Whether the numbers will be meaningful for students is another question."[12] In their opposition to "the numbers," critics
such as these had lost sight of the fact that they referred to college diplo-
mas, not some abstraction that might not hold currency for students.

Such criticism didn't stop or slow our work. Instead we used it as the
starting point for making changes to our approach. For example, the task
forces gradually evolved by moving into the individual colleges, and were
divided into more targeted teams, one at each college, focused on ideas
they had generated and on their implementation at the local level. Once
we had a solid understanding of what our problems were and what we
wanted to do to resolve them, each of the colleges set up separate task
forces focused on the overall initiatives—a move we called Reinvention7,
referring to the different institutions. Incorporating the suggestions meant
getting the work done at scale with teams and stakeholders in the colleges
who worked with the task force members on the front lines.

Ultimately, 20 percent of full-time faculty would work on the Reinvention project; with administrators and students, they would contribute
210,000 people-hours on task forces. As the work continued, we supplemented it with several publicly distributed progress reports. The first,
"Reinvention, Chapter 1," released in spring 2011, outlined the rationale
for change, the framework of the Reinvention process, and the results of
the first phase of work. "Reinvention, Chapter 2," which was released a
year later, outlined the proposed solutions. In 2013, we released a five-year
strategic plan that outlined our quantifiable metrics and expanded on how
we'd measure ourselves along the way (figure 3.3). Through these public
documents, we really shone a light on the institution's new commitment to
transparency and data-driven decision-making.

● ● ●

Along with their implementation plans, the task forces were instructed to
set goals for their strategies. The targets didn't need to be overly ambitious,
but they did need to be quantifiable and measurable. How many remedial
students should be transitioning to credit courses within a year? How many
credits have students completed within their first year? We didn't necessarily
think every goal would be met, and we didn't plan to penalize anyone if they

FIGURE 3.3

City Colleges performance targets

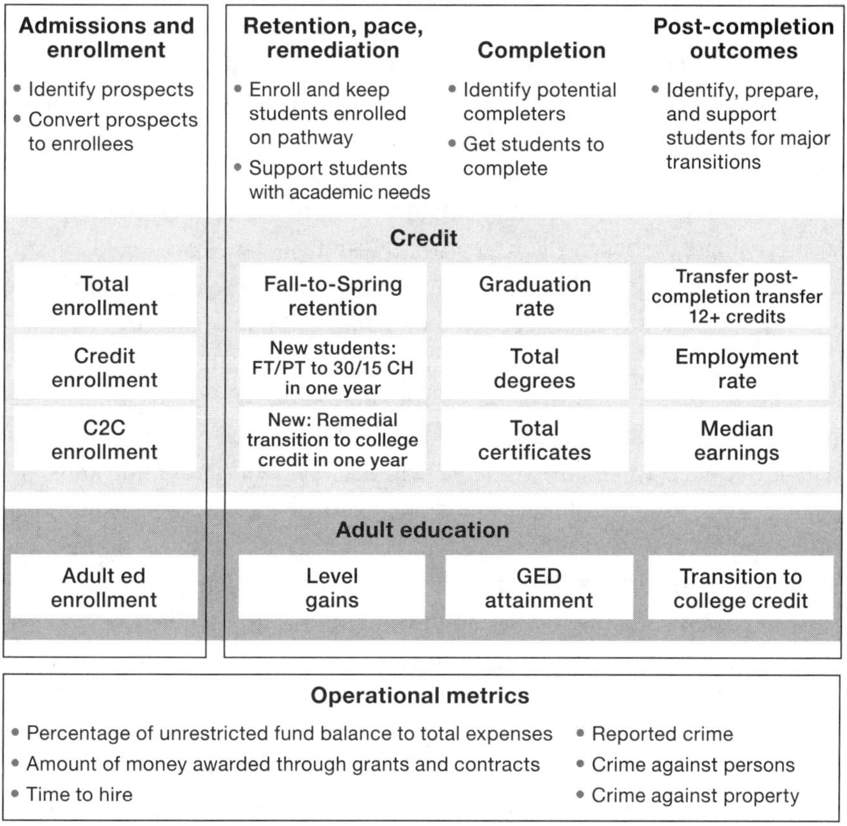

Admissions and enrollment	Retention, pace, remediation	Completion	Post-completion outcomes
• Identify prospects • Convert prospects to enrollees	• Enroll and keep students enrolled on pathway • Support students with academic needs	• Identify potential completers • Get students to complete	• Identify, prepare, and support students for major transitions
Credit			
Total enrollment	Fall-to-Spring retention	Graduation rate	Transfer post-completion transfer 12+ credits
Credit enrollment	New students: FT/PT to 30/15 CH in one year	Total degrees	Employment rate
C2C enrollment	New: Remedial transition to college credit in one year	Total certificates	Median earnings
Adult education			
Adult ed enrollment	Level gains	GED attainment	Transition to college credit

Operational metrics	
• Percentage of unrestricted fund balance to total expenses	• Reported crime
• Amount of money awarded through grants and contracts	• Crime against persons
• Time to hire	• Crime against property

weren't. Rather, our aim was to build a mindset among the task force members and the greater City Colleges community: *We can't improve unless we always know what we are working toward and measure whether we are progressing.*

This focus on data was part of a larger culture shift, and one of the most important changes I would bring to the institution. People's experience and judgment mattered, but now they were just one piece of the equation. No longer would we make decisions solely based on hunches and evaluate our performance based on impressions—we needed to become more evidence-based. We wanted to ensure we remained flexible enough to accommodate individual employers with an overriding interest or demand, but we established a rigorous evaluation process to guard against creation of duplication of high cost programs to benefit a few versus the many students, employers and transfer institutions. Now, if someone asked us to expand a City Colleges program, they would have to show us the number of job openings and wages; there would be no new program if there weren't going to be a certain number of new jobs in the field each year. When professors told us students didn't want to take classes in afternoons and evenings, we asked them to prove it—and once we conducted a usage study, the numbers didn't bear out their assumptions. It was possible to make just about any decision based on data, or the lack thereof.

While the colleges began to implement task force recommendations, we started to see improvements. The first year, we managed a three-percentage-point increase in the graduation rate, which was driven by proactive outreach to ensure students within a year of graduation took the right classes to allow them to graduate. Meanwhile, my leadership team and I were working in the background on our five-year plan. By then the graduation rate for first-time, full-time students was increasing from 7 percent to 13 percent, a nearly fifteen-year high; total annual degrees and certificates granted had increased from just under eight thousand in 2009 to more than ten thousand for the first time on record; and credit enrollment increased 15 percent. This was all great news, but we wanted to get far more targeted about committing to and tracking accomplishments.

The five-year plan embodied the key Reinvention tenets of transparency, accountability, and effectiveness. The main goal of the document was to chart the strategies we would leverage for enhanced success moving forward, much like we were equipping the students with pathway roadmaps. We put in place twenty-four aggressive, quantifiable goals for academic and operations outcomes. We meant for each goal to be challenging—definitely a stretch— but achievable. We aimed to be a best-in-class large, urban community college system by the end of the 2017–2018 academic year. Among our goals:

- The number of degrees awarded annually would increase by another 37 percent, to 5,414.

- The number of degrees and credentials of economic value awarded annually would jump nearly 25 percent, to 11,895.
- The graduation rate for first-time, full-time students would exceed 20 percent.
- 55 percent of students would transfer to four-year institutions following graduation from City Colleges.
- 71 percent of occupational completers would be employed in their area of training upon graduation.
- 12 percent more new remedial students would advance to college-level work within one year.
- Four times as many adult education students would transition into a credit-level course after one semester in GED or ESL programs.

We also had expected—before a state financial crisis would impede these goals—to be strong financially by:

- Ensuring our operating reserves remained at prudent levels of at least 3 percent of annual operating expenses.
- Increasing our funds raised annually from grants and contracts by one-third.
- Ensuring we were able to recruit the best talent in a timely manner, and cut our time to hire in half, to 120 days.
- Reduce reported crimes on campuses, including against persons and property, by 5 percent in the plan's first year.

Toward the end of my tenure, some people would complain that these were not the right measures or targets. At the highest level, this complaint was rooted in not realizing that the most important use of metrics is as a problem-solving tool. We monitored the targets closely to determine where adjustments may be needed—we wanted to be flexible enough to change the way we operated if we were off track, not change the goal we weren't meeting. In short, not meeting a goal often means that there is real problem you need to identify and solve, or that people are not doing what they are supposed to.

Annual scorecards for the district as well as each of the seven colleges measured progress on the five-year plan and were widely disseminated (see figure 3.4). Every other week, the senior leadership team, including the college presidents and vice chancellors, would meet for a full day to

FIGURE 3.4

City Colleges FY2015 Scorecard

▨ Target ■ Actual

Increase the number of students earning college credentials of economic value

The projected IPEDS rate (federally-defined graduation rate for first-time, full-time students who complete within 150 percent of the designated completion timeframe is 17 percent, above the target of 14 percent, and more than double the 7 percent rate when Reinvention began. That projection is subject to verification by the state and federal governments.

The total number of awards (degrees and certificates) topped 11,000 for the second straight year, 18 percent above the target and 50 percent higher than when Reinvention began. In FY2015, City College awarded 4,940 degrees, nearly 700 more than the target and the highest in City Colleges' history, and 6,943 certificates, 19 percent above the target.

Completion within 3 years	14% / 17% ✓
Total number of degrees and certificates awarded	10,070 / 11,883 ✓
Degrees	4,280 / 4,940 ✓
Certificates	5,790 / 6,943 ✓

Retention

Retention is critical to ensuring students achieve credentials of economic value and take advantage of professional opportunities and further education available to them. Fall-to-Spring retention among credit students was at 65.8 percent, reaching 97 percent of our goal.

Credit students Fall-to-Spring retention rate	67.7% / 65.8% 97%

College to careers

College to Careers' success is measured by meaningful and gainful employment. City Colleges reached 95% of its goal for the proportion of students employed in their area of training (58%) and exceeded its goal for median earnings for those students ($33,280). Statistically, these estimates are not significantly different from the targets due to the small sample size yielded by the phone and mail survey methodology. As such, we do not compare year to year on this metric. Additionally, the data reflects at least an 18 month long lag in reporting from the time of graduation to reporting of data. City Colleges is working to identify a way to provide a more robust understanding of this student outcome measure.

Student employment rate in area of training	61% / 58% 95%
Median earnings if employed in training area	32,461 / 33,280 ✓

Enrollment with a purpose

Total enrollment met 92% of our FY2015 target. A commitment to putting students on the pat to success is showing significant progress. Student enrollment in College to Careers programs is far outpacing our projections, at nearly double the target. Credit enrollment met over 97 percent of its goal. Total enrollment was affected by declines in adult education, that have occurred statewide, and continuing education, which has been deemphasized to focus on programs that lead to careers and 4-year college transfer.

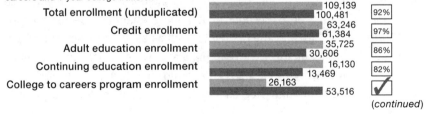

Total enrollment (unduplicated)	109,139 / 100,481 92%
Credit enrollment	63,246 / 61,384 97%
Adult education enrollment	35,725 / 30,606 86%
Continuing education enrollment	16,130 / 13,469 82%
College to careers program enrollment	26,163 / 53,516 ✓

(continued)

FIGURE 3.4

City Colleges FY2015 Scorecard *(continued)*

■ Target   ■ Actual

Increase the rate of transfer to bachelor's degree programs following CCC graduation

The target for transfers was exceeded with 49 percent of credit students transferring within two years of degree completion, up 9 percent since the launch of Reinvention.

Rate of transfer to bachelor's degree programs within 2 years of ccc graduation
43%
49% ✓

Number of fall new students who transfer to four-year institutions after earning 12 credits
736
736 N/A*

*The number of new Fall students transferring after receiving 12 credits is not yet available

Drastically improve outcomes for students requiring remediation

The majority of students who start at City Colleges require at least one remedial course and need to transition to credit work to achieve their goals. In FY2015, City Colleges exceeded its remedial transition target with 38% of students advancing to college-level work within one year of their first semester.

Share of students in the cohort (new students enrolled in remedial course) advancing to college-level work within 1 year of first semester
43%
49% ✓

*CCC exceeds this goal with a few months remaining in the tracking period

Increase the number and share of ABE/GED/ESL students who advance to and succeed in college-level courses

The FY2015 target for students transitioning from Adult Education to college credit was surpassed by more than 15 percent, with nearly 1,400 students transitioning to college credit.

Total adult education students identified in the fiscal year who transition to at least one credit course after one semester
1,181
1,391 ✓

Increase the quality and effectiveness of student services and support

As documented by Complete College America, time is the enemy when it comes to college completion: the longer students take on the way to a credential, the less likely they are to earn it. Students are reaching these key milestones at a higher rate now than before Reinvention. City Colleges reached its targets for both full-time students earning 30 credits within their first year and part-time students earning 15 credits within their first year in 2015.

Percent of students in the cohort (fall first-time, full-time degree/cert. seeking students taking > credit hours) who earn 30 credits within first year
8.2%
8.9% ✓

Percent of students in the cohort (fall first-time, part-time degree/cert. seeking students taking < credit hours) who earn 15 credits within first year
20.4%
20.6% ✓

Improve operational discipline with a focus on high performance standards including excellent financial management

Maintain Unrestricted Fund Balance

By strengthening monitoring and maintaining fiscal discipline, City Colleges met its goal of holding an amount corresponding to at least 3 percent of its operating expenses in reserves.

Percentage of unrestricted fund balance to total expenses
3.0%
3.0% ✓

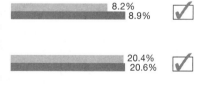

(continued)

FIGURE 3.4
City Colleges FY2015 Scorecard *(continued)*

■ Target   ■ Actual

Grants and contracts

The federal sequester and ensuing slowdown in federal grants have become the new normal, greatly affecting grant activity at City Colleges. City Colleges received more than $30 million in grants funds in FY2015. City Colleges has received a healthy number of the grants for which it applies, but there are fewer opportunities.

Increase the amount of money awarded through grants and contracts  $37.5M $30.9M

Improve Human Resources Practices

City Colleges has revamped its hiring processes by introducing new technology to improve internal data tracking and controls. By employing this new system, City Colleges has exceeded its goal to source, recruit, and hire quality faculty and staff in a shorter time period.

Improve time to hire   120 days ✓
89 days

measure our progress toward the goals. We had modeled in detail where we needed to be against each of the metrics on a daily basis, which allowed for very quickly addressing metrics that were not quite on track. The team would present the outcome metrics—how colleges were doing individually, how the institution was doing compared with last year, and so on. If we were veering off track on one of our goals, we'd discuss what might be done. If one college were outpacing the others, we'd talk about what it was doing right and how those results could be duplicated.

The college presidents knew that their numbers would be transparent, and that I'd be seeing them every week. They were very prepared; they had a solid understanding of what was going well and what they could do differently. The strategy team met with the relevant departmental teams at each college to make sure they were on track to their targets. Beyond the numbers, the goal of the plan was to create a sense of shared purpose across the institution and shared pride over accomplishments. Nobody was penalized when we didn't meet our goals, but we did analyze our goals and progress rigorously.

The data didn't just take the form of pie charts on paper or a Power-Point presentation in a conference room. The data came to life in the daily interactions with students every day by identifying which supports each student would need, thereby allowing staff and faculty to quickly provide more individualized support to students pertaining to their specific goals.

CHAPTER 4

FINANCING AMBITIOUS REFORM

Operations and Efficiency

When you sort through the literature on community college reform, the lectures, the conference panels, and the internet chatter, you'll find a lot of enthusiastic conversation about programmatic and strategic reforms that impact students' day-to-day experiences at college. What you won't find is much discussion of how those improvements are funded.

One of the benefits of bringing in a leader from the business world is that we think about these things all the time—and we act on them. Plans to institute zero-based budgeting, revise procurement, and improve bond ratings don't generate tons of enthusiasm. But it is not an exaggeration to say that bringing fiscal discipline and operational efficiency to City Colleges was one of my biggest contributions, and made many of the other contributions possible.

When I started as chancellor, I noticed right away that the need for more funding was often used, at City Colleges and sometimes nationally, as one of the excuses for lack of effort in aggressively addressing poor outcomes. It was obvious to me, though, that we were not spending the money we were getting efficiently—it takes the same amount of money to provide a relevant degree as it does to provide an irrelevant one. My strategy when I arrived was not just about seeking more money. In fact, there were third parties who had invested in our reforms early on, such as The Chicago Community Trust and The Joyce Foundation. We were extremely appreciative. But I quickly learned that we were not operating the way we needed to in order to effect organizational change and improve service for the students. As I noted in chapter 3, I determined not to solicit or accept money from outside sources until I knew we had our financial house in order and could spend any new money efficiently on revamped programs and capital investments.

This would require a huge change in the way City Colleges did business, one that would yield tens of millions of dollars in cost savings. I embarked on a campaign to improve institutional operations dramatically. This campaign in many ways defined my first few years as chancellor, freeing up funds to invest in students and academics. We tackled human resources, student-facing admissions operations, financial sustainability, and technology. The result set us on strong financial footing for realizing student success goals, and we would be stable enough to withstand the budgetary storm that would take all Illinois higher education institutions by surprise in a few years.

• • •

In looking at how funds were used, the eight Reinvention task forces addressed faculty and staff development, technology, and operations optimization. Just as we did not have clearly defined academic pathways for students, the faculty and staff development task force found that only one in five job families at City Colleges had a defined career path that charted a clear way for an employee to advance to more senior positions. Many of our best employees left because they saw no room for advancement. Job descriptions were often obsolete or redundant with other positions, and there were no performance evaluations. Salaries in some instances were far lower than at other, comparable institutions and in some instances were needlessly higher. Confusing job postings and misaligned salaries also made it difficult to attract and retain talent.

There was no succession planning to ensure continuity in key positions. We needed to be better at identifying talented professionals who could be promoted when critical vacancies arose. The faculty and staff development task force recommended defining job competencies for all staff jobs, organizing positions in better defined career paths within the institution, and aligning duties and salaries with the marketplace. We also needed to better identify talented professionals within City Colleges who could be promoted when critical vacancies arose.

Finally, when it came to sourcing top talent, City Colleges had yet to construct a recruitment sourcebook matching top online, print, and network sources and strategies to our various job families. For example, information technology positions benefit from sourcing from professional associations—websites like Dice; alumni of local university master's programs; and higher education job boards, such as higheredjobs.com. Without a standard, comprehensive repository of employment sources, our recruitment function would treat each search ad hoc, a nonstandard approach to each non-comprehensive search.

In two quick years, under the leadership of Jim Frankenbach, our new chief operating officer (who came from outside higher education), both the faculty and staff development and the operational excellence and optimization task forces and our HR department procured and implemented recruitment and applicant tracking software that hosted an internally developed sourcebook for optimal searches. Service levels for time-to-hire were established, and yearlong processes were tightened to a couple of months. Jobs advertised were competitive due to a normalization of competencies, starting salaries, and schedules.

Hiring, onboarding, and granting tenure to full-time faculty was a particularly sore point in our human resource operations. Our credentialing process for ensuring that faculty met qualifications to teach had many bureaucratic barriers. One or two individuals at district office Academic Affairs department had final say on which faculty would be allowed to teach which courses, often overruling and not consulting the wishes of our vice president, individual college presidents, and sometimes faculty themselves. Making matters worse, there was no standard database for matching credentials in a consistent fashion. All in all, securing of faculty—adjunct or full-time—was a sluggish, nonstandard, discouraging undertaking. Many talented faculty across job families, disciplines, and colleges would ultimately opt out of a City Colleges employment opportunity, as we kept putting our worst foot forward.

For those full-time faculty who did make it through the process, the next hurdle was a capricious tenure process. Illinois legislation establishes that any faculty member employed full-time for three years receives tenure automatically—leaving community colleges a short window relative to other states to determine faculty quality before granting tenure.

Unfortunately, our tenure process did not involve evaluating student performance. Nor was it even about developing faculty. Applicants for tenure were judged primarily on college committee involvement, regardless of those committees' relevance to institutional or student success or their own practice. The importance was not on where the faculty were going or what they were working on, only on assuring that they were properly—which generally meant overly—taxed by the work.

At the conclusion of their third year, tenure prospects had to submit a research paper that was totally self-directed, with minimal oversight, and typically untethered from teaching practice. All tenure projects were evaluated by the same one or two people at district office who did the credentialing, again with little to no input from leaders at the individual colleges, which both faculty and academic administrators sometimes found demoralizing. And a grammatical error killed more than one promising aspirant's dream of full-time faculty employment.

Through Reinvention, several faculty members, in partnership with the Faculty Council, overhauled all aspects of faculty credentialing, tenure, and development. This process was totally led by faculty and modified and officially approved by the Faculty Council.

The recommendation and implementation plans the faculty created were great. The credentialing and tenure processes made a miraculous turnaround. Local leadership was given full authority over both tenure and credential decisions, and district academic affairs administrators used spot checks and database maintenance to verify that the hiring processes followed a standard set of rules, defined by faculty, of what made a given applicant qualified for a teaching position in each discipline.

Tenure was redone entirely. Faculty visited Valencia Community College in Florida, which had an exemplary tenure process, and they replicated and customized some ways to make the tenure process a formative experience. Faculty would be judged on measures of success that included student and peer evaluations and student academic performance; they were also assessed based on their reflections, encapsulated in portfolios steeped in formalized, individualized learning and service plans. Academic administrators in the colleges followed check-in processes each semester and adjudicated the quality of teaching and reflection to understand an individual's performance and promise, in ways that were consistent throughout City Colleges. To date, the tenure process has ensured quality hiring and retention.

Finally, to encourage ongoing reflection and development, we launched Centers for Teaching and Learning at each college. The collaborative atmosphere was designed to provide a positive space for faculty and staff to share ideas, information, and presentations on various subjects. For instance, they could have presentations on city colleges technology, engaging their students through podcast or enhancing digital research in humanities and arts. (Unfortunately, this initiative never developed as fully as the other changes, partly due to budgetary challenges.) We also introduced new technology and technology integration specialist positions dedicated to helping with instructional design and pedagogy.

Just as we needed to invest in student supports, we needed to invest in our own employees, which are the fuel of the institution. In a few quick years, we had clear job descriptions, metrics for performance for faculty tenure, and credentialing processes that made sense. Searches for full-time faculty were now being started a year in advance, and completed months before actual start date, bringing City Colleges on par with our peers in higher education and positioning us to compete for, and to further develop, the best academic talent the best sourcing practices could find. Everything we did was supported by collaborative efforts with our employees. The objective was a shared commitment for student success.

● ● ●

That commitment was something we made tangible a few years into my tenure, when we negotiated a "student success pay" incentive in the new union contracts for administrators, full-time faculty, training specialists, and professional and student services staff. This would replace retention pay, which was an automatic increase of up to 3 percent for remaining at City Colleges from one year to the next, regardless of performance. Under the new system, if we as an institution met our key academic goals on retention, completions, transfer, and career outcomes, the entire group of employees received a bonus of up to 1 percent of their total salary pool, in addition to their cost-of-living increase. Moreover, our 459 part-time adult educators agreed for the first time to set up similar financial incentives to help improve student outcomes. These contracts, alongside negotiated contracts with other employee groups, saved over $15 million in total cost when measured against previous ones. This money could be reinvested into mission-critical student supports, including an overhaul of the student registration process.

We took several other cost-saving steps. We rebid programming that was losing money on the City Colleges television station. We rebid our food services contract to a more financially advantageous one that offered more healthy options. Although we had to work through several challenges during initial implementation, for the first time, we offered online book options (bringing City Colleges into the twenty-first century) for students through a new vendor, which introduced competition and thus significant savings for students.

• • •

Our student support and pathways task force found that our admissions and registration processes were perhaps the most dysfunctional of all student-facing operations at City Colleges. As I've noted, success was focused solely on the volume of students processed, rather than on providing a welcoming experience—and application and enrollment were even failing this simple transactional goal. Seven in ten students registered in person, even though registering online was much easier. Worse, 40 percent had to make three or more visits to register, when other community colleges managed the process in a single visit. If students who attended more than one City College wanted a copy of their transcript, they had to visit each college separately to obtain one. Unsurprisingly, when we polled students, 40 percent reported unhappiness with how long the process took, and one-quarter complained that the staff was unhelpful. And those who took the survey were the ones who had completed the process; many others exited the maze we had constructed before ever registering.

Addressing registration issues right away was critical for three reasons. First, quite simply, we were turning students off who could have benefited from a City Colleges education. Second, the confusion that reigned at registration also meant that students were failing to get the classes they should have, making ill-informed choices, and getting off to a bad start that could jeopardize their success and timely completion. Third, I am a big believer that when you fix a process for one issue, you end up improving other overlapping processes. Instilling a different, more customer-focused way of thinking would hopefully translate to other work, helping improve the student experience and operational efficiency overall.

We pushed on several areas, making the following transitions:

- Adopting scheduling and queuing for registration, which would include an end-to-end analysis of all people who applied.
- Boosting training, and then accountability, for registration staff.
- Rolling out a new online application.
- Streamlining the registration process and materials to be consistent across college campuses and to distinguish between new and returning students, which the current process did not.

In the first year of the new registration process, student satisfaction with registration processes improved. The new online application promoted student choice between colleges, providing them for the first time insight into programs offered across the city. Students would ultimately be able to register more quickly, and with fewer visits, in combination with appointment scheduling technology to set up follow-up advising appointments. First-semester check-ins with advisers would ensure progress along a semester-by-semester education plan, against which, going forward, students could register for courses online and independently.

● ● ●

Our annual budget, $650 million at the beginning of Reinvention, drew one-third of its revenue from city property taxes, one-third (and later one-fifth) from state government, and one-third from tuition revenue. Financial responsibility was a paramount concern—very little is possible or sustainable if the financial side of the house is not in order.

At City Colleges, decades of deferred maintenance meant we had sub-par facilities that impaired teaching and learning and projected a poor image to prospective students, their families, and the community. Poor financial management would mean worse facilities management, which would affect our employees' sense of pride in, and ownership of, where they worked.

Of course many, if not most, of our improvements would cost money. One person suggested, "Maybe we can raise taxes? Or tuition?" I could not justify asking taxpayers or students for more money as long as we had not proved to ourselves that we had extracted all the efficiency we could out of our system. Right away, I could tell that we had not.

Some inefficiencies and their solutions were eminently clear and resulted in immediate redress. There was overspending on employee travel, which we curbed. College credit cards for business purchases were ripe for abuse and thus eliminated. There were dozens upon dozens of requests for contracts for supplies and services. When I received a request to approve a $50,000 fee for a guest speaker, I placed a three-month moratorium on any new contracts and instituted a formal contract request system. It was not that City Colleges didn't have a procurement process; it was just that there had been very little accountability for how taxpayer funds were spent.

Another obvious problem was the administrative redundancies inher-ent in a system of stand-alone, independently accredited colleges. Navi-gating separate but linked entities was hard enough on students—every City College had its own admissions process (and competed for students), and taking classes at more than one or transferring between them meant a whole new set of processes and requirements. But it also created mas-sive inefficiency. Because we had seven colleges, we had seven marketing departments, seven HR departments, seven IT departments—seven of just about everything (which is probably why seven people showed up to the meeting mentioned in chapter 1, when I requested to speak to the head of marketing). On top of that, we had positions across the system whose duties nobody seemed to be able to explain or justify. Each college had a different back-office administrative structure and associated costs. The creation of a single set of institutional goals reflected a huge culture change at City Colleges and occasioned a more centralized approach to back-office administrative functions.

The ultimate aim of these measures was to be able to redirect spending where it could have the most impact: new student services, technology, and improved facilities. So I made the very painful decision to lay off employees. Our fiscal year 2011 budget would contain 311 fewer non-instructional positions—86 vacant jobs would be eliminated, and 225 employees would be laid off. Primarily, the layoffs targeted redundant marketing, human resources, and IT positions across the seven colleges, back-office functions that could be handled centrally by fewer employees at the district office. Sixty people would also lose their jobs at the district office; this included replacing some extremely expensive outsourced IT positions with more efficient and less expensive internal resources and hiring full-time talent. In a memo to all employees, I said that our objective was to spend less on administration and more on education, to free up some of our limited dollars to invest more heavily in our core mission. Under a more unified system, the individual colleges would focus solely on instruction, student support services, and student success. The district office would provide all other support functions, to enable us to operate more efficiently, streamline oversight, and increase accountability.

At the same time I was laying off some administrators, I was hiring others. One of my main personnel priorities was recruiting seasoned leaders from industry: in addition to the new leadership hires that I mentioned in chapter 3, I brought John Gasiorowski on board as our full-time inspector general. His role was to investigate complaints or allegations of wrongdoing or misconduct by employees or contractors that involved or gave rise to fraud, waste, or abuse within our programs or operations. Before joining City Colleges, John was an inspector general for Chicago public schools. Laurent Pernot, a talented and seasoned public affairs professional, was appointed vice chancellor of institutional advancement to bring our disparate communications, development, and external relations functions under one roof so that we could more effectively communicate our reforms and help boost enrollment. He later became my senior adviser, helping to manage that aspect of Reinvention as well as manage various districtwide initiatives to make sure we were implementing reforms effectively and consistently. Rasmus Lynnerup, whose background included a role in the Foreign Ministry of Denmark, joined my team after spending close to six years as a consultant with McKinsey & Company: he replaced Alvin Bisarya as my chief strategist to help drive the implementation of the four reinvention goals. Many of these positions were new (the inspector general previously was a part-time position), which drew more fire from critics: How could this be efficient? While most of these hires took pay cuts to serve, they commanded some of the highest salaries (apart from the presidents) at City Colleges. But I knew that we needed these professionals if we were going to improve processes, coordinate reforms, and put our finances in order.

• • •

It was not just the hires that riled people inside the institution. Simply the fact that we were addressing operational inefficiencies was new to City Colleges. The business-world mindset of efficiency, accountability, and relevancy to the institution felt to me like a conversation that had never really taken place on our campuses. Thankfully, we had the support of Mayor Daley. At a news conference, he said that the new budget, layoffs included, would deliver greater accountability to students. "We can turn this back into a world-class institution," he said, with me at his side.[1]

One major change was the introduction of new business and accounting standards, including zero-based budgeting. From now on, every college, departments, and individual purchaser had to justify every single expense, describing its alignment to the core goals of Reinvention. This had much more than a mere fiscal trimming effect. To the extent a budget is a blueprint of a strategy, we were cementing the primacy of the four goals of Reinvention (increase achievement of credentials of economic value; increase transfer rate to four-year colleges after city colleges completion; improve outcomes for students needing remediation; bridge the gap between adult education and degrees of value). As a result, the requests got smaller, and the achievements greater.

By closing our books every month instead of annually (which was the practice before Reinvention), we became far less prone to financial surprises. It is hard to have your reconciliations or variance analyses current when they are not completed frequently. Financial loss, mismanagement, and bad investment decisions could run rampant. Now, finally, City Colleges began to efficiently track detailed checklists of expenses and understand its cash position in a timely manner.

These basic principles of budget strategy and financial stewardship laid the foundation for cost savings, and the opportunities for savings became quite visible. For example, as part of a comprehensive review to bring benefits more in line with the market, we reduced our benefits liability by more than $1 million annually. We ended sick-day payouts for new nonunion hires, increased health insurance copays and deductibles to be more in line with industry standards, and ended premium-free health care and free lifetime retiree health care for senior leaders. Combined with the step increase and benefits modifications in union contracts, we brought in millions in savings.

Similar to what we had done with our staffing patterns, we needed to find economies of scale in purchasing. Fixing purchasing required us to first end an archaic paper-based twenty-four-step procurement process that did not differentiate between buying servers and buying staplers. Our dozen-step manual workflow was too time-consuming to provide opportunities for meaningful oversight, as staff had to go through as many steps reviewing a paper clip purchase as reviewing a $100,000 equipment purchase. Time was wasted making small purchases, while big purchases were not getting the scrutiny they should have. Meanwhile, it was difficult to get supplies to offices and classrooms when needed. Fortunately, we had an outstanding vice chancellor in charge of administrative services, including procurement services—Diane Minor, who had many years of experience in public-sector work in this area,. Diane worked with the operations task force and eventually made substantial improvements.

To reduce these inefficiencies, the Reinvention operations task force recommended decentralizing approvals for small purchases, streamlining the fulfillment process to cut down on redundancies to have fewer layers of review at both the colleges and district office, and putting in place standing contracts across colleges so we could purchase utilities, software, and supplies at higher volumes.

The operations and capital planning taskforce task force also found that we had no proactive facilities repair and maintenance management system, and that we spent too much, compared with industry standards, on too many ancillary products and services across the colleges, such as printing devices. So we centralized and automated everything from facilities tracking technology to work orders on boilers and roofs to common copier and printing contracts to save $500,000 annually in paper, toner, and hardware.

By centralizing back-office staffing while still providing local staff at each of the colleges, improving HR, hammering out favorable contracts, and streamlining and centralizing purchasing to emphasize high-volume transactions with single vendors, operational achievements in my first three fiscal years netted City Colleges $51 million in administrative cost savings. By 2014, our budget had increased funding for academic affairs by 8 percent, decreased overall operating funds by 2.3 percent, and looked to supplement IT resources through tight capital planning.

• • •

We plowed the funds we saved into reserves, classrooms, facilities, and— perhaps above all—technology. The Reinvention technology task force waded through an ocean of obsolete software, hardware, data systems, and processes. City colleges maintained eleven different websites (one for each college and its satellite), consistent only in their poor design and utility. They were hard to navigate and of little value to students. They reflected no City Colleges brand, no career paths, no way to see how City Colleges programs led to good jobs and careers. Prospective/current students couldn't see a program offered at college B if they were on the college A website.

Poor email contact with students inhibited communication and delivery of critical information to them. Employees did not have an up-to-date email system, so all appointments with outside partners or agencies had to be coordinated by phone. Unlike other modern institutions, we still conducted most business tasks—payroll, room reservations, scheduling, data mining, time sheets—by hand, which ate up staff time and led to mistakes. We did not train our employees on the technology we did have, let alone our students, who did not even have access to up-to-date computers and programs. This was especially worrisome, given that at least 20 percent of City Colleges students had no computers or internet access at home. The findings and recommendations of the task force made it clear that much of our operating windfalls and even more of our capital spending over the next couple of years would focus on technology. The Reinvention technology team would partner with the IT department to design the recommended changes.

In my second year, we launched a five-year capital plan that included $77 million in systemwide academic and student-facing technology enhancements. Interactive smart boards, renovated and modernized science classrooms, refreshed library software and library-stationed computer labs, and state-of-the-art student support centers became commonplace. These paved the way for the new Malcolm X College campus. Located near the heart of the Illinois Medical District, and with state-of-the-art allied health technology equipment and teaching tools, this was also part of the capital plan.

One of the most fundamental technologies funded during this time was data warehouse and analytics capability, along with related staffing investments. We needed the right tools not only to track progress on whether we were improving against our four Reinvention goals, but also to enable faculty and staff to act on that data. Within a couple of years, we implemented state-of-the-art technology and a data warehouse that pushed our most-used data into quickly accessible reports for staff and faculty at all levels to use. City Colleges staff and faculty voted to name this platform "OpenBook," giving principles of data democratization top billing in our ongoing effort to maintain bottom-up participation in strategies, recommendations, and implementation.

Data systems and metrics-driven decision support would ultimately fully integrate into daily operations across the system, from presidents on down to student advisers. This would allow us to monitor and promote admissions, retention, academic success, graduation, and post-completion performance. OpenBook symbolized the intersection of student support, data management, and fiscal stewardship —a cornerstone of decision making around student success financed from operational budgets that embodied our four goals, and from capital planning that looked to the future, and to sustainability.

In 2014, *Campus Technology* named the City Colleges of Chicago as one of several schools to receive its Innovator Award. The magazine praised our technology and strategy departments for "empowering all 5,800 employees . . . with access to a fully interactive reporting and data analytics system."[2]

• • •

Our fiscal discipline would turn out to be even more crucial than we thought in pursuing the work of Reinvention. Whereas the state funded one-third of our budget when Reinvention bagan, eventually Illinois would cut funding to all community colleges, contributing only 20 percent of our funding. City taxpayers and students wound up each contributing a higher share of the operating budget, about 40 percent.

The state's woes got worse. Legislators failed to agree on a budget, and the state cut City Colleges' funding by 75 percent in the 2015–2016 fiscal year. In spite of these cuts, our savings allowed us to stay financially strong. In 2015, we had achieved AA credit ratings from two of the largest rating agencies, with a stated stable outlook. And we still ended the 2015–2016 fiscal year with cash reserves of $130 million.

In addition to cutting direct funding to colleges, Illinois also cut its financial aid, shutting the door to education on more than one-third of our financial aid–eligible students. This had a negative impact on our enrollment and an ancillary effect of denying further revenue to higher education itself. The trend continued, and by the time I left office, the state's folly had yielded a negative credit rating outlook in the BBB range, not far from non-investment grade. After another year of anemic state funding, our cash reserves were rapidly dwindling, in spite of severe cuts and spending slowdowns. Just after I left office, Illinois passed a budget for the first time in three years and began reallocating dollars near pre-crisis levels. But a lot of damage had already been done.

Nowhere was this more epitomized than at my alma mater, Olive-Harvey College. At Olive-Harvey, our outcomes were steadily improving, but we had a severe problem when it came to our transportation, distribution, and logistics (TDL) programs. While we could offer skills in taxi and truck driving, City Colleges simply did not have the kind of high-tech facility and equipment that had redefined companies like UPS and FedEx and was making Coyote Logistics in Chicago one of the fastest-growing business in the country (and sophisticated enough that UPS eventually purchased it to keep an edge in the marketplace). At these corporations, leveraging algorithms and manipulating a computer is as much in demand as operating a forklift. While we already taught the latter, we needed a TDL facility to equip our students with the skills needed for the former.

In 2012, because of Mayor Rahm Emanuel's vision and push for excellence, we were able to come to an agreement with the state to build a new TDL center at Olive-Harvey College, which was located at the confluence of some of the busiest roadways, railways, and airways in the busiest transportation city in the country. The facility would boast computer-equipped loading docks, sophisticated scanning and sorting systems, and a large diesel engine lab that would give students a chance to learn this very lucrative aspect of being a mechanic. This facility would ensure that our students were prepared for one of the 120,000 TDL jobs coming to our region over the next decade. The facility would serve as the distribution center for all goods purchased by City Colleges, giving students real-world experience just feet from their classrooms. Alas, as Illinois slid into its budget crisis, the state halted the project due to a lack of funds, and it was still on hold when my chancellorship ended.

● ● ●

This disappointment aside, the fiscal debacle that all of Illinois higher education endured ultimately highlighted how critical it was that we had planned and launched cost-savings strategies starting early in Reinvention. Even so, lack of funding should never be used as an excuse for at least not trying to address poor performance. Often cleaning one's own house can improve outcomes just as much as, or more than, seeking money from outside it. Unsurprisingly, many Illinois colleges and universities did not fare as well as we did during the two-year budget crisis. Some neighboring and downstate community colleges and universities had no choice but to lay off employees in student-facing positions, including hundreds of faculty members. City Colleges, meanwhile, could weather the storm because of a rainy-day fund of cash reserves built early in the decade from investing in the right resources. But solely relying on our cash reserves could not become the new way of doing business. We would eventually have to make some tough decisions in order to replenish our reserves and continue to invest in our improvements.

We were not always going to be able to afford everything we wanted to do for students. But as we set out to wholly remake City Colleges through Reinvention, while we did face several obstacles, in the beginning, money was almost never the biggest one

CHAPTER 5

A COMMITMENT TO RELEVANCE

Credentials and Careers

Mayor Daley and I launched my chancellorship with a conviction that seemed obvious to me: The primary role of City Colleges was to prepare students for careers (including for those requiring a bachelor's degree and above). This belief would turn out to be controversial—and in fact has been for a century in Chicago and at times nationwide.

From the time Crane Junior College opened in 1911, it was wracked by disagreements over its purpose: Did Chicagoans, including recent immigrants, need vocational education, or preparation for university baccalaureate work?[1] Through the 1920s, most curricula at community colleges were liberal arts–based, preparing students for four-year colleges and universities. In one contemporary survey, 58 percent of California community college students said they were attending "to prepare for the university," while only 10 percent said vocational education was their most important pursuit. Only about a quarter of community college presidents said their institution emphasized vocational education.[2]

The Great Depression changed all that. There was a general feeling that universities were ill-equipped to handle the hordes of new students, and community college enrollment tripled. Given that people needed jobs, and needed to prepare for them, vocational training surged in popularity. By the end of the 1930s, 70 percent of community colleges offered at least one terminal vocational program alongside the academic ones, and states passed laws mandating that dual focus. Meanwhile, universities began to realize they could not afford the tuition losses stemming from turning away students and began refocusing on freshman and sophomore education. As the 1940s neared, only 30 percent of community college presidents saw college preparation as their primary mission.[3] By the 2000s, most community college degrees awarded were in vocational fields.[4]

Our nation's economy relies on community colleges to prepare qualified graduates for careers, in greater and greater numbers. And whether college students seek a vocational certificate or a PhD, careers are ultimately what the vast majority are seeking—including those looking for employment in academic institutions. According to the American Freshman Survey from UCLA, which has been assessing US college students' attitudes for a half-century, this is as true now as it ever was. In 2015, 85 percent of students said they were attending college "to get a better job," the most frequently cited reason, compared with 67 percent who said that in 1971. (That year, "to learn more about things that interest me" was tied as the most popular impetus; now it's number 2.)[5]

What I ran up against was a belief that these two things—as well as other documented motivations, such as gaining an appreciation of ideas—stood in opposition to each other. Some City Colleges faculty felt that offering more vocational (or what I like to refer to as *occupational*) education would push out what they saw as a more important college-preparatory mission. One commenter on a City Colleges–focused blog wrote, "Students deserve a chance to prosper into something better than a skills-based career." Another wrote, "Instead of providing a chance to acquire a higher education for students, they're now being limited to this level of education." I had been vocal about my pride in my trajectory—from City Colleges to a university and then a graduate degree—and that I thought more students, not fewer, should be able to go down that path. As the granddaughter of a woman—a single parent raising five children—who joined the middle-class thanks to nursing training at City Colleges, I also knew the transformative power of occupational education.

The mission I sought for City Colleges comprised all of that. It also happened to be much the same as it was in the 1950s, when the superintendent of Chicago schools described the goals of what was then called Chicago City Junior College in much the same way we'd speak about Reinvention:

1. To develop all students in social intelligence, responsibility and personal culture.
2. To provide the first two years of training for students who expect to complete a four-year college education.
3. To provide professional training for students who expect to continue their education by pursuing professional curricula in higher institutions of learning.
4. To provide semiprofessional training for students who expect to enter the commercial and industrial world.[6]

The problem was, we weren't doing any of that nearly as well as we could or should have.

As one former Illinois lieutenant governor put it, the state's community colleges were creating "revolving doors to the unemployment line."[7] For community college to lead to a career, three conditions must be met: The programs and credentials offered must align with labor market demand; that is, they must be in fields with available, good jobs. Students must be taught the right skills and knowledge for those jobs. And graduates must be set up to progress along a trajectory.

● ● ●

Our first Reinvention goal was to increase the number of students earning degrees of economic value. But for a long time, it appeared that City Colleges programs and course offerings were not based on what had value in the outside world—that is, in the workforce and at four-year institutions.

In the early years of Reinvention, starting around 2012, there was growing acceptance in the community college sector of the idea that to really launch students into a successful trajectory, schools needed to create "guided pathways": setting up clear sequences to degrees and helping students along them in an efficient and focused manner so they could complete on time. Those pathways must be built around the ultimate goal of students: a career. This included students who pursued a liberal arts track. Liberal arts students can of course get good jobs if they earn a degree, but they also need skills. Many will also likely need to go on to graduate school, and community colleges—by saving them thousands of dollars at the outset of their higher education—provide students with an affordable bridge to graduate school.

When I started, nearly forty-three thousand City Colleges students were enrolled in three associate degree programs—associate of arts, associate of general studies, and associate of science—that were typically of little labor market value on their own. And because degrees are only as valuable as the credits and content that go into them, the classes required to complete those degrees must be relevant.

Moreover, in many cases, to get to a good career, students would have to transfer to a four-year school (and hope all their credits transferred with them) and fully understand to what extent their bachelor's degree would be relevant to their prospects in the job market. Yet only about two in five students who got their associate degree were making that leap within two years, and most of those never completed their bachelor's degree. It would be up to us to try our best to figure out where these forty-three thousand students were in their academic study and ensure that more of them transferred—with more credits accepted—to institutions where they would stand a better chance of obtaining the credential they wanted. Ultimately, degrees alone don't transfer; it's the credits from the classes that make them up that do.

Meanwhile, just sixteen thousand students were enrolled in the vocational programs that, as the institution's strategic plan at that time explained, "prepare students for immediate entry into their chosen profession." Data showed there were a lot of job opportunities waiting for graduates who had a certificate or associate degree. An estimated 1,200 information technology jobs were coming to Cook County over the next two years, but we had only 300 IT students enrolled. Only 50 students were enrolled in education, a field that had 1,000 jobs opening annually. Even some fields where we had high enrollment, like nursing, with 1,200 students, were growing enough that City College programs in these fields were not large enough to meet the demand. An analysis we conducted in 2010 shows the misalignment between City Colleges programs and well-paying jobs projected to grow substantially in Cook County (see figure 5.1).

These days, excellent community colleges examine predictive jobs data and offer programs accordingly. Back then, when this wasn't the case, for-profit colleges rushed to fill the gap. At these institutions, workforce relevance to market was the main marketing message. There was a sentiment at City Colleges that for-profits were "stealing" our students. I didn't want to lose students to competitors, of course, and especially not to for-profits,

FIGURE 5.1

2010 benchmarking of City Colleges programs versus earnings and job availability

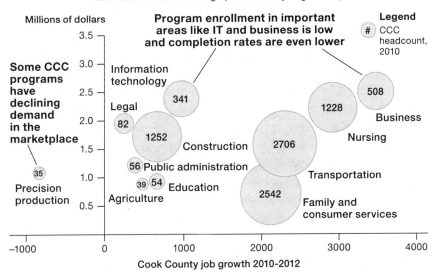

CCC programs are not always aligned with the demands of the marketplace, especially in high-growth areas

Selected CCC programs by Cook County job[1] growth and estimated lifetime earnings

Estimated Lifetime Earnings (Cook County Avg. $1.8M)

[1]Programs included had a job growth or decline of 500 jobs over a two-year time period.

Source: EMSI Occupational Growth for Cook County; June 2010 CCC Headcount.

some of which had bad outcomes—as I had learned personally two decades earlier. The scandal for me was not what the for-profits charged—high costs are not intrinsically bad if great, well-paying careers provide a solid return on the investment—but that students got so little return. That the for-profits were so popular despite their high price and poor outcomes proved a crucial point: Students want to go to a college that they *think* will provide them the skills to get, and succeed in, a good job.

In a report on for-profit colleges, the US Senate's Health, Education, Labor, and Pensions Committee suggested that students might not seek out this subpar option if community colleges and public higher education in general had positioned themselves as a quality, viable alternative for students seeking to skill up in an otherwise down economy. "The existing capacity of non-profit and public higher education is insufficient to satisfy the growing demand for higher education," the report concluded. While the report singled out state cutbacks in funding for this insufficiency, in my opinion community colleges had failed to rise to the challenge not so much because of capacity, but ability. Public colleges that aren't producing degrees of value by preparing students the right way for the right jobs should be held accountable too. They may be more affordable than the for-profits, but regardless of the price tag, you can never get the time back that you lost chasing a dream a college didn't deliver on.[8]

One way City Colleges and many other schools fell short was in helping students shape those dreams. Even when we offered the right programs in high-demand fields, we didn't do much to encourage students to choose them. As much as the country was experiencing a skills gap, it was experiencing an information gap. Students came to us with little knowledge about what jobs were in high demand, how much those jobs paid, what they entailed, and what schooling was required to get them—and we did very little to educate them on that score. "Students often have no idea what opportunities are available to them," wrote Josh Wyner, director of the College Excellence Program at the Aspen Institute.[9] Students' career choices, and thus their educational choices, should be guided by their desires and dreams. But they also must be informed by data.

● ● ●

Even when our graduates succeeded in getting fully credentialed, we heard again and again from employers that some were largely unprepared. They weren't developing the proper critical thinking skills, they didn't know the right technologies, and they couldn't solve problems effectively.

This wasn't unique to City Colleges, or community colleges in general. A 2015 survey commissioned by the Association of American Colleges and Universities asked whether higher education institutions were doing a good job of ensuring that graduates possess the skills and knowledge needed to succeed in advanced positions. Only one-third of employers said yes. Shockingly, nearly two-thirds of students said yes, showing that they did not realize that they were likely to be judged unprepared one day. Nearly 60 percent of students thought they were well prepared to apply knowledge and skills to the real world, but fewer than 25 percent of employers concurred.[10]

Too often, our institution failed to teach the skills required in the real world. This was a problem going back decades. In the early twentieth century, Crane Junior College required that all instructors hold a special teaching certificate and a master's degree and pass oral and written exams, but it didn't require any technical training for those preparing students for industry. At City Colleges, some teachers had never worked in the fields they taught, while some who had industry experience had been out of the labor market for so long that their perception of important concepts could be out of date. I believed City Colleges had an obligation to provide not just students but also faculty better exposure to the real world and establish a mechanism that would continue to keep its employees engaged with external realities.

At effective community colleges, workforce advisory groups meet regularly to offer thoughtful input on curriculum issues, and faculty take their advice. That wasn't happening enough at City Colleges. We offered an IT program that was considered successful internally because it had a relatively high completion rate, but it actually amounted to educational malpractice because it taught the archaic FORTRAN rather than contemporary programming languages. Culinary students were focused on Béarnaise and béchamel. Not only were cream sauces way out of style, but by now, employers wanted new hires to be trained not just in cooking techniques but a range of hospitality skills, almost none of which we were formally teaching.

Sometimes, our graduates weren't learning the necessary skills because we lacked facilities. While nursing students at other community colleges practiced skills in labs that simulated real hospital rooms, with proper equipment, some of our nursing labs—if you could call them that—were little more than regular classrooms with a mannequin on a table. While some colleges had state-of-the-art automotive equipment, one college's facility consisted of a classroom with a few spare parts, but no actual cars.

Time and again, in addition to industry-specific skills, employers told us they were looking for prospective employees with critical thinking ability and appropriate interpersonal, or "soft," skills like professional appearance, timeliness, politeness, and the ability to nurture customer relationships. We were not teaching these, and it was not well understood to be anyone's job at City Colleges. But if you want your students to succeed, it's everyone's job.

● ● ●

When my senior team or I would meet with students, we would ask, "Tell me who you are and where you are in your academic career." Each time, several students said that they had already graduated from City Colleges. "Then why are you here?" we would ask. Routinely, we got a heartbreaking answer: the four-year colleges they transferred to wouldn't accept their credits. Given how expensive it would be to take the right courses there, these students returned to City College for a do-over.

My initial observation upon arriving at City Colleges showed me that the definition of student success had little to do with outcomes. City Colleges simply did not know enough about whether students who moved on to other colleges ever got a degree, much less a job. We tracked, minimally, whether receiving institutions accepted our credits, but not whether transfer students ultimately succeeded. When I became chancellor, City Colleges had signed dozens of articulation agreements with four-year institutions that failed to spell out what was needed to transfer from one college to another in specific programs. As a result, our advisers could not clearly articulate to students what classes they should take if, for instance, they intend to study engineering at the University of Illinois or business at DePaul University. City Colleges was too detached from what students might need or experience after they left us. Yet it was counted as a success if students transferred, even if they didn't get a credential from us first.

This troubled me. Not only had we tolerated middling results inside our walls, we were not paying enough attention to students once they left us. One of our four Reinvention goals was to increase the rate of transfer to bachelor's degree programs, and of course we wanted students to succeed in those programs. For many people, the credential they could get from City Colleges wasn't enough to enable them to meet their goals. Success after transfer was imperative, and part of our obligation not just to our students but to the city and its employers.

As I've noted, even as the first junior college was founded, some educators and administrators felt that community college was an endpoint; others saw it as a step toward a bachelor's degree. Of course, in Chicago and nationally, over time it's been both—what scholars Steven Brint and Jerome Karabel call "this odd hybrid"—with the proportion of programs devoted to one or the other mission ebbing and flowing through the decades.[11]

To me, these distinctions—Endpoint or step toward transfer? Vocational or technical or academic?—were a distraction. No matter what students studied, if we weren't setting up students to succeed at their four-year schools because their credits didn't transfer or they weren't academically prepared or a myriad other reasons, we were failing them. And if we were to fulfill a community college's duty to support students looking for a practical education that would help them in our new skills society, we needed to provide them the opportunity to pursue both vocational and transfer-oriented work. Much of the debate was rooted in academic and economic realities that had largely vanished. Just as a mere high school diploma no longer sufficed to secure a middle-class career, we were now at a point where in many fields—even technical ones—a bachelor's degree, not just an associate degree, was required. They weren't going to be the traditional college degrees, however; they were going to be degrees requiring skills and experience.

To adapt to this new reality, at City Colleges we decided to leave the old dichotomy behind and chart what I call *the third way*—a seamless integration of the vocational, occupational mission of community colleges and the academic, baccalaureate one. These have often lived alongside each other in the same institutions, but we aimed to meld them in the same programs. In this third way, vocational and liberal arts education would not be mutually exclusive, but build on each other. This structure wouldn't just equip students for success, it would bring community colleges newfound relevance for its stakeholders: employers, universities, taxpayers, and government leaders alike.

One of the most significant ways we worked to eliminate the gap between two-year and four-year degrees was to attack the poor state of transfer and articulation agreements at City Colleges, which imperiled the transfer viability of coursework completed by newly minted alumni. By 2015, we had not only inked agreements on guaranteed admissions and credit transfer with popular, high-caliber four-year universities, we had also mapped, semester by semester, the courses students would need to take in their specified area of study, not just in their freshmen and sophomore years but, after associate degree attainment, in their junior and senior years. We were presenting the case to students that earning an associate degree is a great benefit en route to pursuing their bachelor's degree at other local institutions: at DePaul University, where our articulation agreement included a dual admissions program and whose advisers were working with our students even before they graduated City Colleges; at the University of Illinois at Chicago, where we had a guaranteed admissions articulation agreement for some graduates; and at Loyola University, the School of the Art Institute of Chicago, and several others. Our dozen-plus transfer partners worked closely with us to create more than 150 eight-semester, semester-by-semester maps. We built a clear path for information technology students attending City Colleges to continue to the Illinois Institute of Technology, which included a full scholarship and housing—something I sure could have used thirty years before.

With the help of a team of faculty, staff, and industry partners, we began to break down the obsolete barriers between the occupational and baccalaureate missions in other ways too. I tasked the team with one goal: ensure no degree or certificate bestowed by City Colleges was terminal. No credentials we offered should be a dead end. The program portfolio design task force, with the help of external consultants, achieved one of the most significant accomplishments of all the the task forces: to identify whether and how to revamp programs to dramatically increase the number of students who earned a credential of economic value or transferred to a four-year institution following their graduation from City Colleges.

To attack a manageably sized problem—one with the greatest need for improvement and the most potential for quick wins—the initial work in this area was confined to programs that led directly to occupations. McKinsey & Company had worked with us at a deep discount to conduct an eighteen-month study that identified the sectors and jobs within them that would dominate our region over the next decade. The task force settled on six high-wage, high-growth careers in the region—health care (separated into technicians and practitioners), child development, information technology, manufacturing, and biotechnology—and sought to assess how existing City College programs were doing in preparing students for those careers. (These six focus areas would become more defined, and we would add others as we continued our labor market studies and got smarter about the regional job growth.) Employer partners validated those findings and worked with the task force to determine which jobs City Colleges should train students for—nurses, for instance, and not neurosurgeons.

We set out to build a system of what's called *stackable credentials*, a way to break down certificates and degrees into a linear progression that both leads students to jobs and facilitates further advancement. Each certificate should lead into the next: Advanced certificates should lead seamlessly into associate degree programs, and associate degrees should lead into bachelor's programs in that field (see figure 5.2). Stackable credentials weren't unique to City Colleges; at the time, it was a key piece of the toolkit of reform-minded community colleges. But it was new to us.

Child care is a good example of how this works. A basic certificate in child development—made up of an introductory course, two classes health and safety, and hours spent in clinical and observation work—could prepare a student in three to five months to a be a child care worker at $8 per hour. This isn't a great endpoint to aspire to, but at the time there were twenty-five hundred openings for such jobs in the Chicago area each year; and for students just starting out, it was a decent launching point. From there, with another eighteen months of coursework, a student could receive an associate degree in child development, which would qualify him or her for one of the one thousand available jobs as preschool teacher or

FIGURE 5.2   Healthcare pathways: Stackable credentials chart

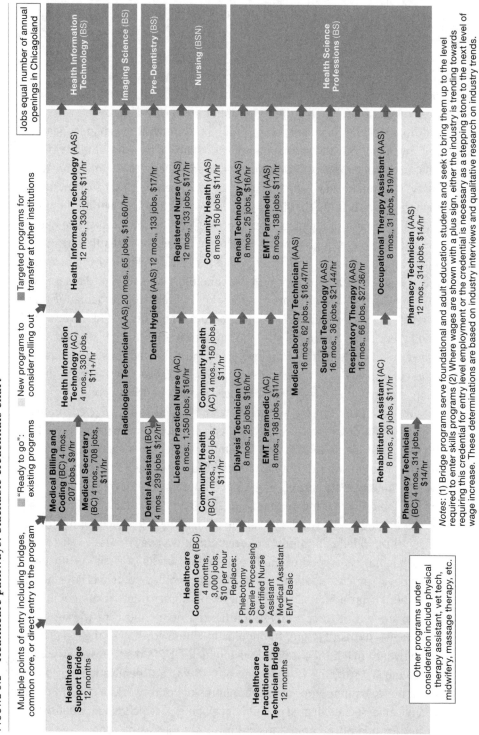

teacher's aide, paying up to $11 per hour. Those who wanted to progress from there could add, with more schooling, the Illinois director credential or a bachelor's degree in child development, which would lead to a smaller but higher-paying pool of jobs (up to $16 per hour).

The key to stackable credentials was ensuring that each set of credits rolled smoothly into the next, without students having credits rejected or skills retaught from square one. The task force proposed stackable credentials in all of the clusters except biotechnology, where the minimum degree requirement was a bachelor's degree. The task force members recommended that their successors analyze the rest of City Colleges' existing or potential programs through a similar prism.

We focused first on health care and transportation, distribution, and logistics (TDL), two fields where many good-paying jobs would be available to graduates and where an associate degree alone no longer sufficed. The lead industry partner in health care who helped us rebuild our programs inside out was Rush University Medical Center, which operates one of the largest and most prestigious hospitals and health-care universities in the country. Like many health-care organizations today, Rush no longer hires nurses who have only an associate degree. No matter how much we improved our two-year programs, our nursing students needed to transfer to another nursing school to get a bachelor's degree if they wanted to work at Rush (and many other hospitals were following this same trend). We had to offer credentials that built on each other no matter where in their trajectory students decided to step off, and work with university partners so that our students could transfer without losing credits.

Like nursing, TDL is both vocational and transfer-oriented. Many think this field is only about driving trucks and moving boxes, beneath what colleges should teach. In fact, both of those jobs can lead to well-compensated careers, and we did train students for those. We also trained taxi drivers; when I first became chancellor, more than 50 percent of the completers in were in the taxi driver–training program. But we aimed to give students opportunities to move beyond these basics. Plenty of other jobs in the industry provide good wages for holders of certificates and associate degrees—someone who earns a four-month advanced certificate in supply chain management, for example, can get a $21 per hour job. And there was significant growth in logistics jobs that required a bachelor's or beyond.

Just step inside Coyote Logistics, and the sea of large screens will help you understand; it does not look like a shipping company, but rather a Wall Street trading floor.

We mapped out a model where after completing an associate degree in distribution and logistics, students would immediately be qualified for certain jobs in the field, but they could also transfer to a bachelor's program in logistics that would give them access to a larger range of higher-paying jobs. For example, we collaborated with Southern Illinois University-Carbondale to facilitate seamless transfer into their sought-after logistics program. For this to work, we had to revamp and integrate our programs from a hodgepodge of credentials that didn't build on each other into a more concerted, cohesive whole.

In the system we built, not only was an eight-week forklift certificate or basic truck-driving certificate good for a job right away, but the credits involved counted toward an advanced certificate in supply chain management, and those credits in turn could be applied toward an associate degree. In the past, a student with a supply chain certificate who had wanted to come back for an associate degree in logistics would have had to start largely from scratch.

● ● ●

A few months into my tenure as chancellor, I was in for a shock. Mayor Daley announced he would not run again. We would have just another six months of working together, but we made the most of it. As he left office in 2011, the graduation rate had increased from 7 percent to 11 percent. It was nothing to crow about, but already it *was* a significant improvement. What's more, proving that institutional improvements benefit all students, the number of degrees awarded—a number that includes all students, regardless of pace and credit load—was also up more than 10 percent.

We had merely laid a foundation, and much more remained to be done. I would just have to do it with a new boss. I knew enough about the front-runners in the race—Chicago attorney Gery Chico, the chairman of the City Colleges board and former chief of staff to Mayor Daley; Rahm Emanuel, President Obama's former chief of staff and a former congressman from the city's northwest side; and the Reverend James T. Meeks, pastor of the

House of Hope church (where I am a member)—to know that one way or the other, it looked like Reinvention was probably here to stay. I just was not sure the same could be said about me. Certainly, there were plenty of people hoping I'd be gone as soon as the next mayor was sworn in.

In February 2011, Chicago elected Rahm Emanuel. When he took office in May, I had just told all the presidents they had to reapply for their jobs, and I half-apologized to the mayor for the controversy he was walking into. But he made it clear that he stood behind Reinvention and told me to double down on what I was doing. The Obama administration was putting community colleges at the heart of America's economic and social agenda, and Mayor Emanuel decided he was going to do the same for Chicago.

Notably, Emanuel was supportive of, and crucial to, one of the more important initiatives we were about to embark on. By the time of his election, my team had the outline of an ambitious project to link our colleges with industry to ensure the relevance of what we taught and the employability of our graduates who chose to go straight into the workforce. It was a grand plan to equip Chicagoans with the skills they needed to grab great jobs in high-growth industries that were going unfilled, and jobs that didn't even exist yet.

In December, in front of a who's who of Chicago businesspeople, nonprofit and government leaders, and journalists—as well as City Colleges students—Mayor Emanuel announced our very big idea. We would call this "College to Careers." It was just one facet of Reinvention, just one way we were working with partners to rewrite the rules of the game for our community colleges so we could help our students write a brighter future for themselves. For Chicago's civic and economic leaders, we knew it would be the most resonant one, and a key indicator of how we were pushing for relevance and excellence.

College to Careers would have a twofold purpose: realigning offerings based on what the region needed and what would ensure our graduates' success, and consolidating programs of disparate quality into one excellent program for each focus area. This vision seemed simple, but it would require us to overhaul just about everything we did, from advising to articulation agreements to capital investment to curriculum. Mostly, it would require changing how we thought. Success would no longer be defined as the mere fact of students enrolling in programs; it would hinge on whether they were being well prepared for good jobs in sustainable careers, in the best possible facilities with the most modern equipment and the highest-quality education. It meant not sacrificing quality for quantity.

In all, City Colleges would focus on seven career clusters (three more would be added later), based on a detailed analysis of which industries would create the most jobs over the coming decade and what skills those jobs would require. Over five years, we would discontinue or revamp forty-one obsolete, low-demand, or poorly structured certificate programs that no longer aligned with or corresponded to jobs or transfer. Among them were instruction in the more than decade-old FORTRAN programming language, a basic certificate and associate degree in horticulture, multiple internally competing offerings for renal technology of highly variable quality, and degrees in courtroom stenography and outdated manufacturing programs. In their place, we launched twenty-two new programs, such as medical billing and coding, quality assurance, factory automation, renal technology aligned to the job market and incorporated into our health-care pathway, CPA preparation (for students who already had a bachelor's), and many more where there was a documented need.

To establish that need, we did extensive data mining, using US Department of Education data, US Bureau of Labor Statistics data, and Cook County employment projections. We came up with four questions we would always ask when evaluating whether to retain or start a program. If the answer to any of the questions was no, we challenged its proposed existence at City Colleges:

1. Does the program correspond to a minimum of fifty job openings per year available to our graduates?
2. Do program graduates earn a family-sustaining wage upon completion?
3. Does the program fit within a pathway from adult education to a bachelor's degree?
4. If "no" to any of the first three questions, does the program serve a compelling community need?

The first three questions were easily answered with the data. Answering the fourth question, where needed, required extensive consultations with employers, professional associations, community organizations, alumni working in the field, and other educators. One example was choosing to retain the mortuary science program to address the need for morticians in Chicago. While the field didn't meet the fifty-jobs threshold, the jobs that it did provide offered graduates a family-sustaining wage and growth opportunities, and there was an employer shortage.

Our data mining showed us that in a lot of cases problems with specific programs were not because there was no need for them. However, the coursework of many programs was not aligned to the job market (whether directly or through a transfer institution) and there was no ongoing monitoring and feedback from employers to update and refine them according to changes in the labor market. For example, we got consistent feedback from employers in the education, IT, and business fields regarding the need for bachelor's degree as the entry-level credential in many areas. In response, we replaced some of our AAS programs with transfer pathways, limiting the use of some programs in these areas to apprenticeship programs with employer commitments to hiring students, and developing new certificate programs that targeted entry-level opportunities not requiring a degree. In our TDL cluster, for example, we added supply chain management pathway programs leading to associate degrees. Within IT, we replaced our CIS (computer information system) program with more relevant stackable programs and transfer pathways focused on web development, added targeted occupations to our computer science programs such as software engineer, and replaced existing networking programs to align with updated Cisco (industry standard) certifications. In business, we replaced and revamped some of our existing accounting programs to target both entry-level jobs such as accounting clerks up to transfer pathways. In our manufacturing program, we learned that jobs being created in this field required more skills than in the past. We added programs on computer numerical control programming, robotics technology, the ability to read blueprints, and learning how to measure parts with high precision.

We also learned from employers the critical industry standards to build our credentials around. For example, at Daley college, our College to Careers center of excellence for manufacturing, students could earn the Manufacturing Skills Standards Council's Certified Production Technician credential, and the machine shop at the college was NIMS (National Institute for Metalworking Skills) accredited. In fact, in 2012, Daley college students earned 10 percent of all NIMS credentials awarded in Illinois, and most students had jobs lined up even before they graduated. Each of our seven colleges would be the official center of excellence for one College to Careers focus. Each would also continue to offer the general education courses needed not just as part of a well-rounded, career-focused program but also as part of a liberal arts–focused associate degree that served as a precursor to a bachelor's. While students would have to travel to the hub campus to take the most specialized courses (courses that required the more capital-intensive investments) in a College to Careers field, they could take the introductory and midlevel courses at any campus. The consolidation would enable us to maintain quality standards and better engage community partners and employers, who often were frustrated about having to connect with several colleges that had several different policies and procedures. It also allowed us to be more strategic about concentrating our capital investments, and we were able to shave $10 million off our initial capital plan while still ensuring our students would be able to thrive in the real world.

Mayor Emanuel told the assembled leaders that we would be launching the first two focus areas the following year: transportation, distribution, and logistics, with 110,000 new jobs forecast over the next decade; and health care, with 84,000 new jobs forecast. The Healthcare program would be located at Malcolm X College on the West Side, near the old housing project where I grew up; and TDL would be at Olive-Harvey, my onetime academic home, on the city's far South Side, in the center of one of the country's busiest hubs of freight, rail, air (the Midway and Gary airports), and shipping (the Port of Chicago). The locations were selected for strategic reasons—to build on the colleges' existing infrastructure and strengths and take advantage of the proximity to potential partners and employers.

Some faculty never came to terms with the changes. We were charged with engaging in discrimination by having what they perceived as high-end programs on the more affluent North Side of Chicago and low-end programs on the South Side. (I do not think I have ever bitten my lip so hard in my life as when I was lectured about failing to understand the plight of minorities.) Yet those who routinely criticized us, say, for concentrating TDL on the South Side—supposedly relegating residents there to what they thought of as inferior professions—had probably never visited the sophisticated, tech-heavy headquarters of Coyote Logistics, and didn't know that according to the US Bureau of Labor Statistics, someone educated in the TDL focus area could look forward to lifetime earnings of $1.9 million.

We were also accused of inconveniencing students by making them travel across the city for some of their coursework. But not to do so would be giving them false expectations of the real world. These were adults who we were supposed to be preparing to go out and make their way in a very competitive society. Expanding their academic opportunities, networking possibilities, and exposure to their city would teach them that they didn't have to be limited to their own zip code to advance. Employers don't locate facilities simply so employees don't need to travel. At the time we implemented College to Careers, one in five students took courses at multiple campuses. To accommodate the need for travel, we launched a shuttle bus that connected to public transportation surrounding the school and linked between schools. (We eventually discontinued the bus when ridership declined.)

The College to Careers Centers of Excellence lineup would eventually include: Business and Professional Services (300,000 new jobs forecast over the next decade) at Harold Washington College, located in the heart of Chicago's business community; Culinary Arts and Hospitality (44,000 jobs) at Kennedy King College, home to the more than century-old Washburne Culinary Institute; Education and Human and Natural Sciences (39,000 jobs) at Truman College; Information Technology (24,000 jobs) at Wilbur Wright College; and Advanced Manufacturing (14,000 jobs) at Daley College, located in Chicago's busiest manufacturing corridor. By 2016, more than fifty thousand of our sixty thousand credit-enrolled students were on a College to Careers pathway. In just five years, and over a period when all the programs were not fully launched, College to Careers generated four thousand documented pair internship or job placements in students' area of training at a pace that was rapidly accelerating, on top of untold success stories as students found jobs through other channels due to their newfound skills and network opportunities.

Our Healthcare focus area provides a great way to understand the College to Careers model. Research showed that eighty-four thousand healthcare jobs were going to be created over the next ten years. We were hardly preparing students to fill them. In 2010, City Colleges had six nursing programs, of which many routinely failed to meet state academic requirements and some were unaccredited—a fact students and community stakeholders were often unaware of—and operated in subpar facilities. We had one program that was outstanding, at Truman College, and its faculty would lead the way, doing an outstanding job in helping to design the new programs and consolidation. But there would never be enough money to develop six programs of that quality, to turn several programs that regulators were threatening to close into best-in-class programs with the kind of modern facilities our partners told us our students needed to be learning in.

We could, however, afford to build *one* excellent citywide program (and couldn't afford not to). The program would be housed in a new building at Malcolm X College, equipped with a virtual hospital tower that emulated every aspect of the health-care delivery cycle. To fulfill their clinical hours and participate in internships and other projects, students would only need to cross a bridge over the Eisenhower Expressway to the Illinois Medical District, one of the largest concentrations of medical facilities in the world, including University of Illinois Hospitals, Stroger (formerly Cook County) Hospital, and the Rush Health System, all of which included extensive education and training for a breathtaking array of medical fields. And some of the best health practitioners in the business would cross the other way to teach at Malcolm X.

Before building the new program, consolidating the other programs into it, or constructing the building, we had to drive to Springfield, the state capital, where we detailed our sweeping plans to get our health programs in shape and begged regulators to give us one last chance. This was a group effort: nursing faculty and administrators rallied across the district to study best practices nationally and among our own colleges. Union leaders at that time made sure there was collaboration between faculty and administrators. Community and industry partners helped us work out the details.

We got a reprieve—and built a great program—thanks to our nursing faculty and health sciences and nursing deans. We attained accreditation for our newly consolidated nursing program, which meant that for the first time in anyone's memory, every single City Colleges nursing student was attending an accredited nursing program—something that employers look for, and that patients should definitely want. In 2010, the Malcolm X nursing program had had a national licensure exam pass rate of 42 percent, well below the state-mandated threshold of 75 percent. When I left, our combined City Colleges nursing program had a pass rate of 92 percent—better than three-quarters of nursing programs in the state.[12]

• • •

As noted, our focus on careers drew opposition. Those whose courses were being eliminated or moved had something to say, even though we tried to find other places for them to teach. There were the geographic complaints. Beyond that, there were opponents who seemed to willfully misunderstand our intentions. By dragging students into career programs to fuel the labor markets, they said, we were shifting away from general education, rejecting the value of English and history, ethics and math. This critique made no sense; the state mandated general education courses as part of a degree, so we couldn't have gotten rid of them had we wanted to—which we didn't! We just got strategic about these as well. We incorporated them into our career programs but also made these requirements specific to the area of study; for instance, a nursing student didn't take the same math as an engineering student, but all students were required to take general education courses. And we knew that employers valued "soft" skills. We tried to explain that we were bringing focus to students' trajectories by clarifying pathways to degrees and careers, and thus expanding their options, not limiting them. We were making sure what we did offer was of value to students at their four-year schools and, yes, their future jobs. Yet some appeared to fear that we were depriving students of more "noble" learning.

• • •

When Mayor Emanuel laid out our vision for College to Careers, he asked the city's business elite to get involved in a very concrete way:

> You all tell me the same thing: from welders, to code-writers, to workers in healthcare and IT services, you need more skilled employees. Companies need workers who make the products, design the products, wire the products, move the products and sell the products—and community colleges can provide them . . . It's unconscionable to

me that we can have more than 100,000 job openings, and close to a 10 percent unemployment rate. It is because I know that we have exactly what we need to answer the challenge, both for employees and employers, and it is right here under our nose: our community college system . . . We are going to remake our community college system into a skills-based, vocational-based educational system . . . We need you to partner with our community colleges—so that their curricula meet the needs of the sectors that power the Chicago economy. I'm not talking about hiring one person or even a partnership. It's more than that. This is about ensuring that the curriculum taught at community colleges provides the skills you need at your place of employment. By making a diploma from our community colleges into a ticket to the workforce, we will make them a first option for job training and not a last resort.[13]

Without the mayor, this would have been a hard sell. City Colleges didn't have the best reputation for reliability or getting things done, and many executives in town had seen proposed partnerships flounder. Businesses and others attempting to work with City Colleges got frustrated juggling multiple contacts and dealing with inconsistent sets of practices and policies between colleges. The frustration was evident at the start of a networking session we had held early in my tenure with Chicago companies—some small, some multinational. I could see the executives literally roll their eyes at the idea of another community college partnership. But the participants became fully engaged and enthused as we began, for once, speaking their language and asking them to do some very concrete things (see figure 5.3). We wanted to understand their needs down to the various skills they were looking for, we wanted help in assessing whether our programs actually corresponded to demand, and we wanted to develop an up-to-date curriculum that would meet their needs for future employees. We asked them to provide internships and job interviews to our students—something they were willing to do once they knew firsthand, finally, that our programs and credentials had value and that ultimately benefited them by helping to train their future workforce.

The curriculum development component was especially critical. Not only did it help ensure our students learned relevant, current skills

FIGURE 5.3

What are and who are College to Careers partners?

**A College to Careers partner can work with CCC
in one or more of the following four ways**

Curriculum review and academic support	On-campus student exposure	Workplace learning	Commit to interview students

- Develop new curriculum with CCC faculty
- Develop an industry certificate program
- Ongoing review of CCC curriculum with CCC faculty
- Donate scholarships

- Industry expos and job fairs
- Work-readiness Workshops
- Mock interviews
- Resume review
- Guest lectures
- Networking events

- Host interns
- Host job shadowing
- Host site visits

- Pipeline of City Colleges students as potential employees
- Utilize CCC's Career Network to post a job or internship
- On-campus interviewing and prescreening

**For each College to Careers focus industry, CCC Directors of Workforce
Partnerships outreach to potential employers, which include:**

- Corporations
- Mid/small businesses

- Professional orgs/chambers
- Nonprofits

corresponding to actual jobs, it gave our faculty unique opportunities for real-world professional development. Through work sessions and visits with industry leaders and practitioners, our faculty would get a chance to have very close connections with employers that helped us transfer knowledge in a very effective way.

Several companies at the meeting signed up to be part of the effort. With the help of Mayor Emanuel's relentless recruiting efforts, our roster of industry partners would grow to two hundred and include some of the country's most notable companies, such as Accenture, the lead partner in our IT focus area; Aon Insurance in Business and Professional Services; and Kimpton Hotels in Culinary Arts and Hospitality. Nearly every community college in America has industry partners. But often those partnerships exist primarily on paper. We wanted—*needed*—to do things differently.

We put in place a new infrastructure around College to Careers, including a dedicated workforce development team at the district office led by Meredith Sparks Ament, an extremely talented manager and graduate of the Harris School of Public Policy, and staff in new positions who monitored external job and skills data and worked closely with College to Careers deans and presidents at each college to ensure that we collected partner input and effectively nurtured partnerships over time. With Accenture, we developed a soft-skills curriculum that was integrated into various programs and courses. Our partners helped us with the design of new facilities, so that we were building for the needs of tomorrow, not yesterday or even today.

Key partners joined College to Career advisory councils. Even after the initial reinvention of our programs, they met regularly to help us update programs and curriculum, advise on capital upgrades, donate equipment, and provide thousands of internships for students. Several directors and associate deans had jobs dedicated to making sure the insights of our partners translated into actual improvements in curriculum and programs at each college.

The mayor cautioned us against being a "short-order cook"—starting programs in response to the narrow needs of a single employer. Sometimes this happened if there was a critical or special need or a growing demand we could get ahead of. But we aimed to focus primarily and systematically on industry-specific, as opposed to firm-specific, skills that would be portable if a particular business moved or relocated—an approach that required the input of several employers in a given field instead of one. It was exciting to have *Fortune* 500 companies that normally compete vigorously against each other come together in a room to discuss what skills were common across their industry, and help us ensure that our students would succeed.

Really, our way wasn't a third way. If community colleges were going to stay relevant—dare I say competitive?—engaging deeply and meaningfully with employers and four-year institutions was the *only* way.

CHAPTER 6

SETTING THE "GPS"

Structured Supports for Students

Offering the right programs and the right pathways is a great start—but it's just a start. We also need to support students, one by one, to make sure they are choosing the right programs and classes and getting the support they need, whatever form that takes.

When I enrolled in City Colleges in the early 1990s, I was not sent to an admissions officer or an adviser, but to the business office. Although all of my encounters with the staff were pleasant, I was tossed back and forth like a hot potato from the financial aid window to the bursar's window and back . . . and back . . . and back again. Once my financial aid application was complete and that transaction was done, I was handed a fat academic catalog to decipher. All I had to go by was a list of suggested courses that weren't specific to a program and didn't necessarily count for credit at the universities. I very seldom saw an adviser throughout my entire time at Olive-Harvey. Nobody encouraged me to take a full course load, even though going part-time would increase the time and cost it would take to get my degree; or to do better in my Intro to Business class because it was directly related to a future in computer science; or to take only classes that would transfer to the program I was planning to enroll in at a four-year college.

I thought this was normal until I got to the Illinois Institute of Technology. It was a rude awakening. Even though I had earned a 60-credit associate degree from the City Colleges, only half my credits transferred, and I had to redo my sophomore year. But at IIT, I was well supported despite the rigorous curriculum, thanks to tutors for every class and an adviser I saw several times, who helped me understand exactly what classes I needed to take to complete my degree as quickly and inexpensively as possible.

City Colleges was, and is, filled with students facing the same obstacles I once had to overcome: struggling financially, uncertain of higher education conventions, and lacking experience navigating massive bureaucracies. Fifty-six percent of City Colleges students are the first in their families to go to college. For these reasons, it was especially tragic that the system was for so long not set up to adequately guide and support students.

• • •

As students returned to campus in late August 2010, we met with leaders of the Student Government Association to ask them what about the City Colleges experience needed the most attention. One of their greatest frustrations was that the colleges didn't actually provide guidance—not about their courses, nor about what would come after that. "Advisers just suggest courses," one typical comment went, "but they don't connect it to my program or graduation requirements." Another said, "Faculty just push their own classes. They aren't telling me what I need to take to graduate. I don't think they even know."

Given that we had only one adviser for every nine hundred students, this was not surprising. During peak periods, advisers saw more than fifty students a day, and faculty members pinch-hit as advisers, without any training.[1] It wasn't their fault that students were not getting the guidance they needed. But it wasn't okay either.

Now that we were digging into the data as a matter of course, we could see how many problems originated with the lack of advising. Many students came back to us after graduation to take courses they never knew their destination university required. Others had enough credit hours for an associate degree—or even a bachelor's—but they were the wrong credits for the degree they sought. While some students told us they took a meandering path by choice, most were simply bewildered by our manifold and complex offerings and requirements, and most never saw an adviser.

Complete College America, an organization whose board I would soon join, demonstrated in a report called *Time Is the Enemy* that this was a national crisis. On average, associate degree students took 79 credits to earn their 60-credit degree. In part because of that, it took full-time students 3.8 years to graduate with an associate degree meant to take two years; for part-time students, it took five years. Giving students more time only marginally improved their chances of graduating.[2] In fact, research showed that by lingering too long in our halls, students were drastically decreasing their odds of ever finishing any sort of degree. Even among the few who did graduate, drawing out the time to complete also substantially increased the cost. On top of that, financial aid runs on a ticking clock, and taking courses that don't move you forward can jeopardize your financial aid eligibility.

The problem was clear. Students were getting lost inside our walls. The solution was clear too: we needed to provide students with clearer roadmaps to graduation and beyond.

We adopted a system of "guided pathways," an approach that was gaining popularity at reform-oriented community colleges. The strategy was simple. We needed to work with students to understand their preferred destination based on relevant data and choices, then give them a semester-by-semester map of major courses and possible electives to get to graduation in a timely manner. It was no accident we called this "GPS" (Guided Pathways to Success); we joined Complete College America in using this navigation metaphor to visualize the role of pathways within an educational institution. This work was started by our Reinvention7 college-based task forces, which comprised full-time faculty and staff members with expertise in the subject areas for which we would build our GPS system (by 2016, faculty members made up more than three-quarters of Reinvention teams).

A consensus is growing among community college experts that guided pathways are a necessary precondition for student success. According to the Community College Research Center, "complexity and confusion" reign at colleges where students still choose from among a huge array of "cafeteria-style" course options. Without clear direction and structure, students take too many unnecessary courses and have lower chances of completing.[3]

Many community colleges across the country are being recognized for their work in this domain. At Lake Area Technical Institute in South Dakota, winner of the 2017 Aspen Prize for Community College Excellence, students choose a technical program and proceed through two years of fixed sets of courses with the same group of classmates. The completion rate is among the nation's highest, more than 70 percent, and 99 percent of graduates are either employed or continuing their education within six months of completion.[4] In 2012, City University of New York started a new community college from scratch, Guttman, where students choose from just six associate degree programs, and all but six of their 60 credit hours are preselected for them. The college is off to a fast start, with a three-year graduation rate of 49 percent.[5]

Deciding to adopt guided pathways was the easy part; implementation would be quite arduous. Before establishing pathways, we had to harmonize our course offerings and requirements. In some programs, when I arrived at city colleges, seven colleges meant seven different sets of courses and seven set of prerequisites and requirements (even if it was the same program) making the system hard to navigate for students taking classes at more than one campus. In a few instances, we even found classes that were prerequisites for *each other*, making it impossible to get into either one. So we spent much of my first two years synthesizing one catalog for the district. Numerous advisers, with input from faculty, spent several months developing a course layout for each pathway, term by term.

Once the pathways were created, they had to go from living on Microsoft Word documents and Excel spreadsheets to undergirding an information technology system that would ensure students stayed on track at every step. We identified the four-year colleges that the greatest number of our students transferred to, and a few that were not on the list but should have been because they aligned with our College to Careers program offerings. We met with university leaders so they would better understand our reforms and programs and so we could do an inventory of which existing or yet-to-be-created courses a student should take to transfer to these institutions as a full-fledged junior solidly on track for her or his intended major. One shining example of this was the University of Illinois at Chicago. We achieved such a high level of precision in aligning our curriculum that there is now no difference between coursework for a pre-engineering student at UIC and a pre-engineering student at City Colleges destined for UIC. In five years, we signed more than 150 articulation agreements with four-year institutions, each outlining which courses students needed to transfer from City Colleges to that college or university with no credit loss.

Once we ourselves understood what it took to get into the four-year schools and what credits would be accepted there, we mapped the ideal course sequence for our students not only to graduate from City Colleges but also to thrive at the college or university best suited for their academic and career goals. Just as we had done in the early days of Reinvention, we brought together faculty from across the institution to chart the pathways together. Working with Reinvention staff, they identified not only the appropriate courses for various credentials, but also the correct sequencing for both classes specific to programs and those for general education requirements. Just as for College to Careers, we evaluated which programs were truly relevant and pared those that weren't. As part of the Pathways project, faculty, with the help of four-year partners, simplified our program offerings from eleven hundred complex and sometimes redundant options to just three hundred. Faculty also worked across disciplines to suggest electives for each pathway that both reinforced the pathway work and broadened students' horizons beyond it.

To fully realize the potential offered by community colleges and to maximize their time and money, students must be able to progress toward individually declared goals, along structured degree plans that embed the liberal arts in the form of general education requirements. Doing so is not undermining freedom of choice. Making systems easier to navigate, eliminating non-relevant programs or reducing the proliferation of elective courses (especially when they don't transfer), is work to promote alignment to educational and business needs. These are protections for students of limited means, protections from wasting their dollars on coursework they do not really want or that cannot transfer (much as many of my own courses did not transfer from City Colleges to my four-year destination more than thirty years ago).

By 2016, all credit students who declared a program and intended to continue their education beyond City Colleges were put on a semester-by-semester pathway with a corresponding map that included the courses at their transfer institution that would lead them to a bachelor's degree. Each pathway allowed students to track how much time and how many courses they had until graduation and also mapped important actions for them to take, such as "meet with your adviser this semester." With the pathways came a list of suggested extracurricular activities and internships that would augment students' academic work and increase their appeal to universities and employers.

We developed an online pathway-finder tool, as well as a new portal that enabled students to explore program options. The portal brought eighteen different systems under one roof for ease of access and use for both students and employees. The pathways tool introduced students to each of the ten focus areas—the original seven plus construction technology (because we had a current facility focused on construction trades) and natural and human sciences (which we incorporated at Truman college, which was our education College to Careers center of excellence)—as well as the pathway we created for students who had interests outside of the focus areas and a pathway for those who were undecided. (Failing to declare a major reduces the chances a student will graduate in a timely fashion, so at least we wanted to make sure that undecided students were taking courses that would give them credit toward any program.) Students were given information about various careers in any field, including the required credentials and coursework, jobs available, expected earnings, and potential to move from one stackable credential to the next. A prospective Advanced Manufacturing student, for instance, could in three semesters earn an advanced certificate that could get him or her a job as a computer numerically controlled machine tool programmer, paying nearly $30,000. Or the student could continue to an associate degree and then a bachelor's to become an industrial production manager, with a starting salary in the mid-$50,000s—or a dozen options in between (see figure 6.1). An adviser would share a program map that laid out all the necessary courses and actions.

Over time, just as employers had come on board as committed College to Career partners (and were now posting their jobs on our newly designed website), the improvements we made in pathways and academic alignment cemented our relationship with four-year partners. As with the College to Careers group, they had faith in our programs, since they had helped

FIGURE 6.1

City Colleges 2017–2018 academic catalog

CITY COLLEGES OF CHICAGO 2017–18 ACADEMIC CATALOG

ADVANCED MANUFACTURING

PATHWAY: Manufacturing Technology: CNC Machining

Visit your College Advisor, ccc.edu, or your college's Transfer Center for more information.

This is an **example course sequence** for students interested in earning a degree in Manufacturing Technology. It does not represent a contract, nor does it guarantee course availability. If this pathway is followed as outlined, you will earn a Basic Certificate (BC) in Quality Assurance (QA), a Basic Certificate and an Advanced Certificate (AC) in Computerized Numerical Control (CNC) Machining, and an Associate in Applied Science (AAS) in Manufacturing Technology. One course will satisfy the Human Diversity (HD) requirement, and is labeled with an (HD) in the sequence below.

The AAS degree program in Manufacturing Technology offers the technologies required for maintenance mechanics in the manufacturing or service industries and covers theory and practical projects. The program is appropriate for career changers, high school graduates, general education diploma holders, and machining workers with a need to enhance their careers.

The Advanced Certificate program in Computerized Numerical Control is designed for the study of the basic principles of machine tool technology incorporating basic computer applications to the manufacturing industry, including CNC programming and computer integrated manufacturing (CAD/CAM).

DEGREE CODES:
AAS 770C AC
(CNC) 725
BC (QA) 729
BC (CNC) 724

Choose your courses with your College Advisor.

Communications and mathematics pre-credit requirements. Placements based on current placement instrument, ACT or department chair recommendation.			College-level courses that can be taken while in pre-credit courses.	
ENGLISH PLACEMENT	READING PLACEMENT	MATHEMATICS PLACEMENT	REQUIRED PROGRAM CORE	ELECTIVE COURSES
☐ ESL/FS Writing	☐ ESL/FS Reading	☐ FS Mathematics I	☐ Manufacturing 111	☐ INTDSP 102
☐ ESL/English 98	☐ ESL/Reading 99	☐ FS Mathematics II	☐ Manufacturing 112	
☐ ESL 99	☐ ESL Reading 100	☐ Mathematics 98	☐ Manufacturing 139	
☐ ESL/English 100	☐ Reading 125	☐ Mathematics 99	☐ Manufacturing 141	

SEMESTER-BY-SEMESTER PROGRAM PLAN FOR FULL-TIME STUDENTS
All plans can be modified to fit the needs of part-time students by adding more semesters.

D	ACᶜⁿᶜ	BCᵠᴬ	BCᶜⁿᶜ	SEMESTER 1	CATEGORY	ACHIEVEMENTS & NEXT ACTIONS
•	•		•	Manufacturing 111–Machining Processes I (3)	Required Program Core	
•	•		•	Manufacturing 112–Machining Processes II (3)	Required Program Core	
•	•	•	•	Manufacturing 139–Print Requirements and Quality Assurance (3)	Required Program Core	DO THIS–Meet with advisor to discuss academic goals and plan coursework
•				Manufacturing 141–Manufacturing Materials and Processes (3)	Required Program Core	*Required for BC 724, but not the AAS
•			•	Interdisciplinary Studies 102–Career Development and Decision Making (1)	Required Program Core*	
•				Art 103–Art Appreciation (3)	Fine Arts & Humanities	
				16 CREDIT HOURS		

D	ACᶜⁿᶜ	BCᵠᴬ	BCᶜⁿᶜ	SEMESTER 2	CATEGORY	ACHIEVEMENTS & NEXT ACTIONS
•	•		•	Manufacturing 138–Introduction to SolidWorks (3)	Required Program Core	ALMOST halfway through Associate in Applied Science degree
•	•		•	Manufacturing 140–CNC Fundamentals (3)	Required Program Core	DO THIS–Meet with advisor to confirm plans
•		•		Manufacturing 142–Geometric Dimensioning and Tolerancing (3)	Required Program Core	
•	•	•		Manufacturing 143–Advanced Metrology (3)	Required Program Core	
•	•	•		Mathematics 125–Introductory Statistics (4)	Mathematics	
				16 CREDIT HOURS		

D	ACᶜⁿᶜ	BCᵠᴬ	BCᶜⁿᶜ	SEMESTER 3	CATEGORY	ACHIEVEMENTS & NEXT ACTIONS
•	•		•	Manufacturing 123–CNC Milling Operations and Programming (3)	Required Program Core	COMPLETION of Basic Certificate in CNC Machining COMPLETION of Basic Certificate in Quality Assurance DO THIS–Go to Career Center to explore both continued education and employment options DO THIS–Mid-term check-in with advisor
•	•		•	Manufacturing 137–CNC Turning Operations and Programming (3)	Required Program Core	
•	•		•	Manufacturing 144–Wire Electrical Discharge Machining (3)	Required Program Core	
•	•			Manufacturing 207–Introduction to MasterCAM (3)	Elective	
•		•		Manufacturing 104–Statistical Process Control (3)	Required Program Core	
				15 CREDIT HOURS		

This semester map was last updated on February 28, 2017.

(continued)

FIGURE 6.1
City Colleges 2017–2018 academic catalog *(continued)*

ADVANCED MANUFACTURING			
D	AC°NC	BC²A	BC°NC	SEMESTER 4	CATEGORY	ACHIEVEMENTS & NEXT ACTIONS

D	AC°NC BC²A BC°NC	SEMESTER 4	CATEGORY	ACHIEVEMENTS & NEXT ACTIONS
•		Manufacturing 191–Industrial Electricity (4)	*Required Program Core*	
•		Manufacturing 292–Principles of Mechanisms (3)	*Required Program Core*	COMPLETION of Associate in Applied Science degree in Manufacturing Technology
•	•	English 101–Composition I (3)	*Communications*	COMPLETION of Advanced Certificate in CNC Machining
•		Sociology 207–Sociology of Sex and Gender (3)	*Social & Behavioral Sciences*	
•		History 215–History of Latin America (HD) (3)	*General Education (HD)*	
		16 CREDIT HOURS		
		DEGREE MINIMUM: 62 CREDIT HOURS // PATHWAY TOTAL: 63 CREDIT HOURS		

D = DEGREE // AC = ADVANCED CERTIFICATE // BC = BASIC CERTIFICATE ⚑⚑⚑⚑⚑ Programs offered at: ⬤⬤⬤⬤⬤⬤⬤

Only the Computer Numeric Control Machining BC (724) is offered at Wright College

design or validate them. Some universities came to value our students enough to admit them sight unseen if they had a certain GPA. After the Illinois Institute of Technology offered a full-ride scholarship to up to a dozen City Colleges students each year, the number of students transferring from City Colleges to IIT more than tripled. DePaul not only offered slots to our students, it gave them access to its advisers while they were still at City Colleges; the number of transfers there doubled. UIC and City Colleges established the Guaranteed Admissions Transfer program, which allowed our students to apply and be accepted at UIC as early as their second semester with us. Once accepted, they could access various UIC resources, from the library to lab time. Transfers to UIC were soon up nearly 50 percent.

This played a significant role in boosting the percentage of students transferring to a four-year institution from less than 45 percent to nearly 50 percent, and increasing the earnings of students working in their area of training by 7 percent.

• • •

With all the pathways in place, however, we had more work to do. A map doesn't do much good if you don't know how to read it. If we were to meet any of our four major goals (increasing the number of students earning credentials of economic value, increasing the rate of transfer to bachelor's degree programs following city colleges graduation, improving outcomes for students in need of remediation, increasing the number of adult education and ESL students who advance to and succeed in college-level courses), we realized, we needed to build the right systems and processes—both human and virtual—to help students navigate the system and keep them on track. We upgraded our existing student management system and acquired and adapted off-the-shelf student support and data warehouse systems, IT advancements that completely revolutionized how we engaged, tracked, and advised students.

Support needed to start the minute students walked through our doors, or even before then. It used to be that simply enrolling in City Colleges required a Sisyphean effort. Early in Reinvention, meetings with admissions and other college staff, focus groups with students, and some "secret shopping" of our registration processes made clear that while we were technically an open-access institution, we were really only accessible for students with unlimited time and patience. New students, depending on their preferred college, could have to fulfill up to fifty-two steps and six visits to campus before they could sit in their first class.

Our new portal gave us the ability to collapse most of the steps into a single visit, and we developed an automated education planner. By visiting the City Colleges website, students could not only apply and register—with a progress meter indicating how many tasks they had completed toward successful registration—but also explore career options, view tuition costs, and build sample class schedules. Once they were enrolled, the system would remind them of upcoming administrative deadlines and adviser appointments and alert them to any academic or financial holds they might have, with links to where to get help for such things as transferring credits in from another institution. We also created a call center and trained phone advisers who could answer general questions for all seven colleges and counsel students about program and career choices even before they were assigned an in-person adviser. The phone advisers also were trained to make outbound intervention calls to students in a variety of situations.

I heard criticism about the call centers—that they were a waste of money. But our colleges were overwhelmed with day-to-day phone calls, and this was intended to relieve some of that burden and better serve students at the same time. A major part of reform is innovation. You evaluate along the way. Sometimes things work, and you scale them. Sometimes they don't, and you adjust or discontinue them.

I believed it was unacceptable for even one student to miss completing a degree or certificate because of something we did not do or information the student didn't receive. Early in Reinvention, even before the call center was in place, we adopted a case management system and and early alert system, called Grades First, that would look at grades, attendance, and other factors and notify advisers and administrators when a student was falling behind and needed support. This alone was a huge leap for us. Yet it wasn't long before that felt insufficient—both to meet our four Reinvention goals and hold people accountable for them. We were blessed with an extraordinary manager, Charles Ansell, who worked for Rasmus Lynnerup, my chief strategist, and would take our technology tools for student support to the next level. A former research analyst and IT project manager, Charles was a senior leader in our strategy and academic governance unit, and put in place a system at City Colleges to track every one of our potential completers and make sure they received the help they needed. We tracked every metric biweekly, from student success to financial health. This started with Excel spreadsheets for every student close to graduation and regular phone calls with deans. Once we rolled out our new portal, it was easier to integrate the data. This granted us a level of sophistication for advising that was unthinkable a few years before.

Degree audits, which measure whether a student is on track to satisfy graduation requirements, were once conducted manually in what was an arduous and error-prone process. Now they were automated, tracked by staff and students themselves. Students in the cohort we were tracking were flagged if they had yet to receive a degree audit. They were flagged if they did not have an education plan or pathway (usually because they had not yet chosen a program). A computer alert warned them if they were trying to select a course outside their pathway. As mentioned above, all credit students were monitored for any warning signs that their progress was slowing or was somehow hindered by financial or academic holds, so that we could identify problems and work through possible solutions with the student. D's and F's at midterm triggered automated phone calls suggesting tutoring. At certain midpoints—15 and 30 credits to graduation—students were reminded to adhere to their academic plan so they could finish on time.

Importantly, these technological tools were paired with an intensive effort to increase and improve advising. An automated phone call or an online alert might trigger a conversation, but it was human beings who would need to conduct those conversations. Ideally, advisers help students understand the importance of choosing the right pathway early, as well as a course load that's as full as possible. They're the ones learning what is happening in students' lives, inside and outside of school, that is affecting their ability to succeed, and pointing them to the right supports. When an alert comes through that a student is taking a course she failed before, the adviser calls to ensure she gets help this time around. If a student withdraws the first week of class, the adviser calls to find out why. If a student fails to purchase books, the adviser calls to make sure everything is okay and remind him to place the order.

What we had created was a system of genuinely high-touch advising, coupled with technology that allowed students to serve themselves. What's more, advisers were required to meet face-to-face with students, have them complete education plans, and update those plans. This aggressive case management was made possible because we hired many more advisers. Through savings generated by eliminating administrative redundancies, we lowered the student-to-adviser ratio from 900:1 to 350:1, and at some colleges it was even lower than that.

The commitment to student success was so intense that even college leaders were focused on individual students. Advisers would phone administrators with detailed potential scenarios that individual students could experience and jointly plan out what would help them succeed; college presidents, deans, and even I were involved in discussing how we could help individual students who were veering off track.

As we dug into the data and learned more about why students weren't persisting, we added more layers of support. We opened a career center at each college to help students select and move through the right pathways, connect them with jobs, and help them fine-tune resumes and prepare for interviews. In every college, we also added a transfer center, veteran support center, and wellness center where graduate students in psychology provided mental health counseling for social and emotional issues and students were directed to community resources and social service agencies. At every college, we added a math emporium that paired online coursework with human assistance, and each president analyzed data to see where students were struggling and added tutoring centers specific to their needs.

• • •

One huge obstacle to effective course completion was our scheduling of classes. Sometimes the problem was that the courses needed for a particular pathway were spread throughout the week, rendering them inconvenient especially for students who worked. Sometimes the issue was that courses were bunched together, so that courses for a particular pathway conflicted. An administrator once told me that we simply did not have the physical space to add new sections based on the new pathways. It turned out that, as was common throughout the institution, sections were concentrated in popular windows of time—popular for faculty, that is.

An analysis of space utilization showed that some colleges offered almost no classes in the afternoons, on Friday, or on weekends. One held nearly half of all its classes between 11 a.m. and 2 p.m. on Monday through Thursday! When I asked why we scheduled classes this way, I was told that's how the students wanted it. But there was no data to support that assumption.

In fact, when we surveyed students across the seven colleges, we found that one in five students was dissatisfied with our class schedule, and the biggest scheduling challenge cited was "day and time the class is offered." Students were interested in early-morning and evening classes. And 55 percent said they would be likely or very likely to take classes between 2 p.m. and 4 p.m., the time when we offered the fewest classes. Even if students didn't like taking a course in a certain time slot, they said they would if the class were required for graduation. We presented this data to college presidents and senior administrators so they could shake off the conventional wisdom and start spreading offerings throughout the day to be more convenient for the students and to help them with timelier completion of programs.

We also made it possible through our online portal for students to specify their preferred days and time to come to school, based on whatever else they were juggling in their lives, and their preferred location. Then, the system did two things. By cross-checking those preferences and the course schedule, it spit out the optimum registration options for the student to take the classes they needed that term to progress as quickly as possible toward graduation. It also gave us added intelligence to get smarter and better at deciding which sections to offer when, and where. This, we hoped, would help us pave the way for the next frontier of City Colleges: the ability for students to enroll in their entire program from day one (whole-program enrollment) and maintain the same schedule term to term for the duration of their chosen program (predictive scheduling). These two innovations would, when implemented, remove large obstacles to juggling school and work schedules.

Another attempt to help get students into the classes they needed came in 2015, when we stopped allowing students to register for classes as late as the first day of the term. When students waited this long, there wasn't always space in the classes they wanted, and when there was, they often didn't have time to see an adviser or buy books and materials. Late registration was also hard on instructors, as it meant we didn't always offer the right number of sections. We moved the registration deadline one week earlier, embarked on an all-out communications campaign, and even advised students who missed the new deadline into a twelve-week session that started a little bit later that fall.

Another crucial initiative in our attempt to speed time to completion was to get more students to take a full load of courses, now that we had fixed so many of the systems problems and made it easier to navigate through pathways. Because the US Department of Education defines full-time status as 12 credit hours for financial aid purposes, most full-time students at City Colleges took only 12 credit hours per semester. But to complete an associate degree in the standard two years, students have to take 15 credits a semester—typically one additional course. Some students could make up for lost time by taking the additional course over the summer, but in cases where they couldn't apply their federal financial aid to summer classes, this was not an option.

In 2012, the University of Hawaii system began a campaign called "15 to Finish," leading to a 40 percent increase in the number of students taking a full load each semester—and the finding that those who took more hours actually did better academically. A similar effort at Adams State University in Colorado resulted in a 14 percent increase in credits attempted by semester, without an adverse impact on outcomes. Neither of these institutions had incentivized students to change behavior, nor had their student demographics changed. Rather, they trained their advisers to promote full course loads and implemented marketing campaigns high-lighting their benefits.

Before registration in fall 2014, we embarked on our own "15 to Finish," with a twist. Like the other colleges, we launched a campaign to encourage students to take a full course load, including strategies like automated phone calls to students taking 12 credits suggesting they enroll in an eight-week mini-course. Significantly, we also built in a financial incentive: students who took 15 credit hours in at least one semester could take one summer class at no cost, thereby further speeding their potential completion. In the fall 2014 term, the number of students taking 15 or more credit hours was 38 percent higher than in fall 2013. Even though these students were taking more hours, they earned 64 percent of their attempted credits, compared with 60 percent for full-time students taking 12 to 14 hours. The 15-hour students also got a higher GPA than the full-timers taking fewer hours and persisted to the next term at a higher rate.

Still, across all full-time students, credit hours increased by only 0.2 hours per term. I was concerned that there might be other barriers that were preventing our "15 to Finish" initiative to be as successful as it was at other institutions, especially since this approach already had proven to be a game changer for other institutions. So in 2015, I challenged my team to investigate other potential roadblocks.

We decided to provide a key incentive to take a full load through the way we structured tuition. Illinois's funding level for community colleges had been declining dramatically, resulting in a $30 million loss for us over five years. Revenue shortfalls of up to $60 million were forecast for our 2015–2016 academic year. With the prospect of more cuts looming, we took the painful step of increasing tuition, on average $225 a semester for part-time students and $200 per semester for full-time students. Tuition would be $1,069 per semester for students taking two or three classes, and $1,753 for students taking four or five classes, without any additional fees. This would be coupled with an immediate spending cut of $30 million, driven by decreases in nonessential spending, such as travel and supplies, and a dramatic slowdown in hiring.

We had been the only community college in the state that had not raised tuition or fees in five years, which we were able to accomplish by enacting administrative efficiencies. Up to this point, due to our relentless focus on financial stability, we had been able, though painfully, to absorb most of the state's funding cuts, but now the cuts were threatening our ability to keep delivering the successes of Reinvention for our students. In education, unlike most business, there are very few options for creating additional sources of revenue. So like most of the other Illinois colleges, we were faced with the need to increase tuition. At the same time, we asked ourselves, what if we could eliminate the cost uncertainties for students while also helping them complete faster?

The concept was flat-rate tuition across nearly all programs. There were two main components: First, we would completely eliminate nearly all fees (around 150 of them), many which served as barriers to College to Careers programs with the strongest projected job growth. Lab fees could run into the thousands of dollars for programs like culinary sciences or some natural sciences. Now 15 credits of, say, dental hygiene would cost the same as 15 credits of English. Removing fees also made for more transparent pricing, as students who just calculated their expected costs based on the per-hour tuition rate often had sticker shock (and even dropped out) when they saw how much their cost jumped with fees factored in. From a business perspective, a flat rate would help us better project our revenue.

Second, we would eliminate economic barriers to students taking more hours by creating a flat tuition structure for full-time and part-time students. Under our existing tuition system, a full-time student taking five courses per semester (or 15 credit hours) paid 25 percent more than one taking four courses. For part-time students, taking three courses cost 50 percent more than two classes. Some students were taking fewer classes for personal reasons like work or family obligations. But if the barrier to taking more credits, and thus progressing faster toward graduation, was economic, I wanted it removed as much as we could. We set a tuition for full-time students that was the same whether they took 12 or 15 credits, and likewise set a fixed tuition for part-time students. We had done so much work to address structural problems through pathways that it was easier for students to take a full load. Now that extra class to get students to a full load was essentially free.

Though they kept saying they were concerned the state budget crisis would force layoffs, some critics blasted the new tuition structure, claiming it would drive away part-time students, whose tuition would increase more, percentagewise, than for full-time students. But even with the increase, our tuition remained within a full-time Pell award, and 60 percent below what neighboring community colleges charged Chicago residents. Not only didn't the tuition drive away students, including part-timers, student outcomes improved. A few months after the change, we saw an immediate bump: 20 percent more full-time students were taking 15 or more hours, and the course success rate, completed credits, and GPA all were up. Part-time students also were taking slightly more hours, although their academic outcomes were largely unchanged. By spring 2017, two years after the new flat rates were implemented, the shift in course-taking behavior was even more pronounced. After being flat or down for several years, the number of credit hours part-time students registered for increased by half a percentage point, compared with before the new tuition structure. The average number for full-time students was up by nearly as much, to an even 14 hours per semester. And the GPA for both full- and part-timers either increased or held steady.

What eventually hurt *everyone*, especially our students, was the state budget crisis.

• • •

As part of the movement to increase completion, community colleges had started giving credit where credit was due, so to speak, and we joined the effort. We began awarding what are called *retroactive degrees* to students who didn't realize they had met the requirements to earn a degree and had left City Colleges without it. Before Reinvention, City Colleges didn't know these students had earned these degrees either, but the regular degree audits that we initiated made it clear.

We also started granting reverse-transfer degrees to students who transferred from City Colleges just a few credit hours short of graduation. With the student's consent, we applied credits from their four-year institution and awarded them an associate degree. They might be able to leverage the degree for more earnings if they worked while pursuing their bachelor's. If they wound up transferring to a four-year institution but didn't earn their bachelor's, they still had an associate degree to show for their years in college.

Both of these practices are not only common sense, because they bring true economic value to our students, but they are also considered best practices in the national movement for student completion. In 2013, the nonpartisan Institute for Higher Education Policy, funded by the Kresge and Lumina foundations, reported on the success of a three-year effort involving 61 institutions in nine states that awarded both retroactive and reverse-transfer degrees. Retroactive degree audits meant that thousands of students in many states either were granted degrees they were eligible for or were successfully encouraged to return to school and complete.[6] In 2015, the Bill & Melinda Gates Foundation and the Lumina Foundation completed an effort to solidify reverse-transfer partnerships between community colleges and four-year institutions in twelve states, including Illinois.

Every student who leaves a community college having earned a degree should get it, and students who leave without a degree should be offered the opportunity to complete it if they earn additional credits after transferring. Some critics say such efforts are attempts to manipulate the completion statistics to make the institutions that grant them look better, but these retroactive degrees are not awarded unless the necessary credits have been earned (per the federal guidelines of how the graduation rate is calculated, in most cases, the degrees don't count toward the graduation rate). Students who have put in the time and hard work deserve a credential to prove it, regardless when they earned it.[7]

• • •

The intensity of our efforts to increase degree completion through clear pathways and supports has clearly paid off in a quantifiable way—a way we call the Reinvention Bump. We add up the number of degrees awarded each year over and beyond the pre-Reinvention level, and multiply that by the $423,000 in lifetime earnings an associate degree is projected to bring a person, compared to just a high school degree.[8] That $423,000 can be the difference between owning a home or not, being able to send one's children to college or not, or enjoying a secure retirement or not. In all, the Reinvention Bump is worth in excess of $5.6 billion in added lifetime earnings for Chicagoans. That's a big reason to be proud, but also a big reason to sustain and grow these efforts, because there are so many more people who need and deserve the kind of opportunity that comes from being helped down a clear path to success.

CHAPTER 7

ON-RAMPS AND BRIDGES

Remediation, Adult Education, Early College, and the Star Scholarships

Community colleges tend to serve those of our country's students with the greatest disadvantages. Even within those colleges, some populations have especially intense needs. When we centered two of our four Reinvention goals on our least-prepared students (improving outcomes for students needing remediation, and bridging the gap between adult education and degrees of value), I didn't know these were among the hardest problems for community colleges. But I knew we weren't setting ourselves up for easy wins.

Nationally, nearly 60 percent of students who enter community college require some form of remediation—that is, they are not prepared to do college-level work in math, English, or both.[1] At City Colleges, that number was 90 percent. It's a fact across all colleges that students who arrive with remedial needs are less likely to complete, and our numbers showed that to be distressingly true. Only 28 percent of students requiring math remediation and 45 percent of those needing English remediation ever made it to college-credit work. Students who needed remediation in three or more subjects had only a one-in-ten chance of ever earning any sort of credential.[2]

That doesn't even count the students who needed remediation but never even made it into one of our classrooms. When students register for City Colleges, as at other community colleges, they take placement tests that determine whether they're ready to jump right into college-level work or need remediation. We found that just under half of students who tested into what are called "developmental" courses failed to register for a class that semester, and two years later, most had still not registered. We reached out to some of these students, who told us how discouraged they were to finally make it to college—often, it was the first time for anyone in their family—only to be told they would essentially have to spend more time in high school.

City Colleges was spending more than $30 million in direct costs each year to provide remediation but had not made a dent in the problem. I'm not sure if anyone knew the extent of the problem, as the institution had not tracked outcomes specific to remedial students. I knew that if we were going to help large numbers of students access the middle class and help bridge the skills gap in Chicago, we would have to solve the remediation problem. In his 2011 speech, Mayor Emanuel put it this way: "Let's be candid: Most community colleges offer students what they should have learned in high school. Too often, they provide remedial learning to compensate for gaps in their education. That is not why our community college system was established."[3] Community colleges often fail to live up to the "college" in their name because they are too busy teaching students skills they should have learned in high school.

But the students didn't learn them. Although community colleges spend a lot of time teaching what should have been learned in high school (remediation), they too see low success rates—sometimes traditional remediation just doesn't work. For many at City Colleges, the discussion ended there. One-quarter of the twenty-thousand or so Chicago Public Schools students graduating high school each year went to City Colleges, and people expressed their frustration: "What do you expect us to do with these students?" someone once blurted out in contract negotiations. "There's nothing we can do for them."

It was indeed true that many of our problems—including, in part, our low graduation rate—were caused by a domino effect that may have been triggered by the poor performance of some primary and secondary schools. It did seem unfair to hold community colleges and their faculty members accountable for problems that had their roots outside our doors. But this is what it meant to be an open-access institution. Community colleges had originated in Illinois a hundred years earlier to provide access to opportunity for a wide swath of Americans, and these were the students walking through our doors. If we were to help these students and make headway on retention, completion, and other measures of student success, we could not throw up our arms and simply place the blame elsewhere. We needed to become partners with Chicago Public Schools, which was working on some great initiatives that we could benefit from and become a part of. (Unfortunately, the improvements that Chicago Public Schools were working on weren't going to happen as fast as everyone wanted, and they wouldn't have any effect on the students we were already committed to.) Put simply, we had to start seeing ourselves as one seamless institution from Chicago Public Schools to City Colleges.

• • •

We started with a small initiative in 2011. Rather than attempting to revamp courses, Daley College, in conjunction with the Reinvention team, began a pilot in which it supplemented some developmental courses with mandatory tutoring and online support for students grouped in small learning communities who took multiple courses together and held small-group discussions after class.

Within one semester, we saw what looked like dramatic results. Students in the cohorts with enhanced supports were more than twice as likely to pass introductory remedial classes with a C or better than non-cohort members. The success rates were almost as high for more advanced remedial courses.

Had we struck gold? It turned out we had not. When we scaled the initiative across the entire college, we saw only very modest gains. The year after the pilot was first rolled out, the percentage of students "graduating" to college-level work did increase from 30 percent to 32 percent, but then outcomes plateaued. There seemed to be two reasons. First, because we had built the extra-support cohorts by seeking volunteers, we were likely helping the more committed students with better study habits. Second, because we had left the remedial courses themselves largely untouched, the other students were not reaping many benefits from our efforts—or theirs, for that matter.

Staff from Daley college, the Reinvention team, and the remediation taskforce went back and thought about how and why students were getting slotted into remedial courses in the first place, and what that experience felt like for them. We realized that among other things, our placement process was imprecise and often placed students too low. Our new model was centered on the idea that, from day 1, *college should feel like college.* That meant welcoming and treating treating remedial students in the same way we treated those registering for grade-level courses. One thing we did was begin a pilot project called Level Up with the Chicago Public Schools, which provided new graduates with computerized mini-courses in English and math to help them pass the remedial placement test once they arrived at City Colleges. The initiative reduced the time spent in remediation by 1.2 semesters on average; overall, 94 percent of participants experienced at least one grade-level increase in English, and 57 percent of students experienced level gains in math. Across the board in English and math, participants were successful at more than twice the rate of nonparticipants. Again, we thought we had struck gold, only to find some of the same issues with scalability. We simply couldn't figure a way to make this program work both academically and financially for over 100,000 students.

As part of a new student experience effort we launched at Wright College in fall 2015, students took new online and math assessments, developed by our own faculty, that were more accurate than previous tests and included noncognitive skills in addition to the traditionally tested cognitive skills. These tests allowed faculty to spend more time assessing qualitatively where students truly were from a preparedness and study skills standpoint. In short, standardized test don't tell the whole story, and they sometimes even tell the wrong story.

We chose this as the first pilot because Wright was at the time our college with the largest enrollment; we figured if we could master this at Wright, it would be easier to scale to the other colleges. Although at times they may have doubted some of the evidence from similar efforts in other parts of the country that had produced dramatic results, the English and math professors at Wright still stepped up and put a lot of energy and time into rethinking developmental education, and staff from the other colleges worked with them to learn along the way.

When students did get placed into remedial courses, we didn't want it to feel like, much less actually be, an academic death sentence. We put in place corequisites in math and English—remedial booster courses taken alongside an intro college-level math course, sometimes taught by the same professor—so that students could get over those hurdles early and remove barriers to other courses, like biology or literature, that they were ill-equipped to succeed in or were barred from because they had not taken or passed those threshold courses. Also, because even remedial students had to choose a pathway right away, they could take just the courses that were appropriate for their pathway; for instance, a student bound for a culinary certificate didn't have to take the same math course as a student bound for an engineering degree. Some worried this was a form of tracking, but students who changed their focus could easily take a more advanced math class.

It used to be typical that there were not enough remedial courses for the students who needed them, so they would be placed in courses like art that did not have an English or math prerequisite. This stemmed from the fact we had allowed students to register as late as the first day of class, so it was hard to plan the right courses. Our new requirement that students register no later than one week before the first day of the term (see chapter 6) allowed us to test and support all the students more appropriately.

After the revamped approach to testing, students fit into one of three groups. The college-ready group would take college English and math in addition to other courses on their pathway. The second group, at the low end of college-ready, took college-level math with corequisites and intensive English college prep, as well as eligible pathway courses. In addition, they took a course called College Success, which helped them with academic planning and study skills, and had access to a full deployment of tutors and advisers. For the third group, the least prepared, we piloted enrollment in College Success as well as a new 12-credit-hour course that provided an intensive dose of English or math. The goal was to have everyone enrolled in 15 credit hours, both because the data showed that students with a full load got better grades and because it put them on track to a more timely graduation.

This new approach yielded immediate gains. After that first fall, the percentage of new Wright students who had completed, were enrolled in, or were eligible to take a college-credit course the next semester was up nineteen percentage points in math and six percentage points in English. While the gains were more modest than the ones we had seen a few years before at Daley College, they were in fact more radical and sustainable because they were spread across all students, were built into the core college activities, and were the results of newly redesigned coursework aimed at students with the greatest remedial needs.

We rolled the approach out to all the other colleges but Daley, which continued its experiment (an experiment that would later confirm our concerns about scalability). By 2017, transitions out of remediation within one year jumped from 31 percent to almost 51 percent. One college even saw an increase of thirty-nine points.

● ● ●

Every year, City Colleges educates about thirty-two thousand students who aren't (at least initially) seeking a degree. Rather, they are learning the basic skills necessary to attain a high school diploma and speak English. For most students in what's typically called "adult basic education," that's the end of their academic journey. However, since we were committed to launching *all* our students into a productive career, we needed to give them more.

From the very start, Reinvention faced a two-front challenge in our GED and ESL programs. First, enrollment was down. On a practical level, we didn't want to lose students and the funding that came with them. But more importantly, we knew the number of people who could be benefiting from our services hadn't gone down, and we wanted to reach them.

In addition to these two challenges, the adult education task force found that just about every one of our colleges offered registration materials only in English, and the English version was hard to understand even for English readers. There was very little advising, even when students had multiple no-shows. So we needed at least bilingual materials and an enhanced registration and advising process. The student-to-adviser ratio in adult education was 3,371 to 1, advising offices were often closed at the times when adult education classes met, and there was no advising presence at our satellite locations and off-sites (these were run by third parties, typically, community-based organizations), where a significant portion of adult education took place. City Colleges staff seldom visited those off-sites, and we provided little and inconsistent guidance to those providers in terms of quality and outcome expectations.

Using Census data to map the potential adult education population, we saw that our locations didn't sufficiently reach the universe of likely students. Of the 330,000 adult Chicagoans without a degree, only 45,000 enrolled in a GED or ESL program somewhere in the city. We engaged on a large-scale effort to shift locations within the networks of existing providers and create new collaborations with new providers in key neighborhoods.

For the first time, we audited the quality of instruction and facilities of our third-party providers and shut down some subpar sites. But we opened more, including thirty new sites between 2012 and 2013, in previously neglected areas. Per the task force recommendations, we hired more staff, including advisers; revisited hours and locations for advising; and developed a set of standards and guidelines for all adult education locations that would be coupled with enhanced training and oversight. Progress would be tracked via a metrics dashboard, and we would boost awareness of state and federal policies by having more consistent communication with regulators at all levels. Enrollment grew for the first time in several years.

Managing enrollment was the easy part. The far bigger challenge we had created for ourselves was to turn adult education from an endpoint to an on-ramp. The relevance we were working so hard to infuse into our career programs was just as germane here. Merely completing an ESL or GED program is an important and necessary goal if a learner wants to move on to gainful employment or further his or her education, but it alone has limited economic value, as most careers required some amount of college. Our fourth goal of Reinvention was to bridge the gap between adult education and degrees of value. We aimed to not just turn our ESL and GED students into college students, but successful College to Careers students.

To make this happen, the task force proposed expanding an existing GED FastTrack College Prep course and two new transition bridge programs (see figure 7.1). At the time, accounting was the only viable pathway for this population. But even if all our GED students wanted to be accountants, there were virtually no job openings for students with an Accounting Clerk basic certificate.

This would ultimately lead to students earning occupational certificates as part of our GED program. The first was Career Bridges, which prepared students to pass the GED in the context of a career field, like health care, logistics, or culinary arts. Students in Bridges committed to 18 credit hours per week, which included a free College to Careers class on their chosen pathway. Coursework was tailored to the pathway: a reading assignment might use a statement of need from a transportation client; a math problem might require students to calculate and measure the right dosage of a given medication. Not only did students move from adult education into their desired College to Careers program better prepared and engaged, along the way they also earned certifications that demonstrated skills and motivation to employers.

The second new program was the Gateway Scholarship, through which City Colleges subsidized tuition for students who had just completed adult education to take college coursework. It also provided a suite of supports to assist students in the transition to credit courses. This would redefine our adult education as not an endpoint but as an on-ramp to college. More than two thousand students, including many immigrants, would eventually receive the Gateway Scholarship. Almost half persisted in the following semester.

A great partner for our team as we reinvigorated adult education at City Colleges was Women Employed, a nonprofit organization. Our teams worked hand in hand over multiple years to drive improved outcomes for our students. One of our joint focus area was developing relevant curricula to allow students to understand the career and academic pathways they could pursue—including bridge programs to ease adult education students' entry into those vocations. When I left City Colleges, our materials, which we gladly shared, had been downloaded more than eight hundred times by organizations to teach in their own programs. Penn State researchers would select our bridge programs as one of three in which to understand the use of career pathways for adult education students.

In the 2016–2017 school year alone, more than fifteen hundred students took part in these two transition programs. All told, we increased the

FIGURE 7.1

Code City Colleges' bridge program

FY12	FY13	FY14	FY15	FY16	FY17	FY18
• ICCB Shifting Gears grant prioritizes stackable credentials, transitioning students into college • CCC begins to develop Bridge framework accordingly • BNA health care bridge launched at DA	• Health care bridges launched at six campuses • Bridges launched: TDL at OH • Culinary at KK • Manufacturing at DA • Transition Specialists hired at all colleges	• Business bridge developed; not completed due to lack of pathways at HW* • Manufacturing closed at DA at end of fiscal year	• Healthcare consolidation causes Bridge enrollment to drop by 53% • Early Childhood Ed bridge launched at TR • iCAPS launched at OH	• Bridge structure standardized, tied to pathways • Healthcare bridge opened at SCLC (first bridge at a satellite)	• IT bridge launched at DA, WR, HPVEC • CCC chosen by Penn State to be featured in study as one of three top Bridge programs nationally • Curricula revision started for all bridges	• BNA bridge launched at MX • Manufacturing / pre-engineering relaunch • Bridge-to-Basic-Certificate campaign to be launched at all campuses • CCC curricula downloaded ~800 times by other adult education programs
92	403	535	493	392	431	261 (SU17, FA17)
Student enrollment						

*At the time Accounting was the only viable pathway with virtually no jobs openings in market for students with an Accounting Clerk BC.

Note: DA=Richard J. Daley College; KK=Kennedy-King College; HW=Harold Washington College; TR=Harry S. Truman College; MX=Malcolm X College.

number of adult education students transitioning to college from about five hundred in 2010 to more than eighteen hundred in 2016.

• • •

Mayor Emanuel and I often discussed the need to ensure that our incessant push for success did not sacrifice access. We both were committed to ensuring that *everyone* had a shot at a City Colleges education. In his second term, President Obama began pushing the idea of free community college for all. The political calculus and resulting dynamics in both Washington and Springfield meant the proposal didn't quite get the traction that had been intended. And so, as he had done with College to Careers, Emanuel had already decreed that Chicago would take matters into its own hands. He called a meeting to let me know we would offer free college to deserving Chicago Public Schools students.

This would be a perfect complement to our early college offerings. Under the dual-credit program, Chicago Public High Schools high school students could take City Colleges courses for free in their school with specially trained teachers. Under our dual-enrollment program, they could register as City Colleges students and enroll in courses alongside college students. To do either, students had to be declared as college ready, which meant testing at 21 or above on the ACT.

These programs, especially dual enrollment, demystified college. Whether students ultimately enrolled with us or elsewhere upon getting their high school diploma, they did so already knowing they could handle what college threw at them. Under Mayor Emanuel, we increased that program more than tenfold, to serve more than four thousand high school students.

Working in concert with the mayor's senior staff, we sketched the outline of a free college program. Students who graduated from Chicago public high school with at least a B average and tested college ready would have three years at zero cost—no tuition, free books—to earn a City Colleges associate degree. The scholarship would be open to all, regardless of immigration status. The mayor said this was a very cost-efficient ticket to the middle class for anyone who received it. He believed that students who worked hard should be rewarded with a fair shot at a college education, regardless of their parents' income, and parents should not have to go deep into to debt to send their children to college.

After receiving congratulations for devising such a wonderful program, we refined our thinking: Was "college ready" the right yardstick, especially when so many high school graduates came to us requiring remediation? In our minds, a B average, rather than an ACT score, should carry the most weight, because it was a sign of the student's drive and tenacity.

Our team locked themselves in a room and came out with an unconventional solution: we should replace "college ready" with the concept of "completion ready." Because the scholarship gave students three years to earn their two-year degree, and because we were finally making headway with remediation, we should put our money where our mouth was if we believed our reforms were working. That meant taking in students whose academic record might be a bit spottier and who would place into remedial courses but whom we could help get to college level in a year and graduate in another two. The students with B averages had put in the work. We would have to do the same to ensure they had all the chances possible to prove themselves in college.

In the fall of 2015, we welcomed the first group of almost one thousand "Star" students at City Colleges. They would be followed by another thousand the following fall, and we were forecasted to bring in that many the third year. Universities were enthused about the program, and the mayor capitalized on this by enlisting them in the Star Scholarship Partnership, under which more than a dozen local universities would offer partial or full rides to Star students who graduated from City Colleges with a 3.0 GPA.

Both programs have been a success academically. In 2017, thanks to the early college programs, more than two hundred Chicago Public Schools seniors graduated from high school looking ahead to less time in college and smaller college bills because they had earned a semester's worth or more of college credit at City Colleges while in high school, for free.

By the end of the spring semester 2017, we had our first 175 Star scholarship graduates, 70 percent of whom were first-generation college students. They had reached that milestone in two years at a higher rate than the rest of our student body did in three years. Based on the Star cohort's progress, our data team forecasted that these students would outdo the average national average community college graduation rate by a factor of two.

When we held a reception for Star scholars and their parents, one African American mother of five thanked us, half laughing and half crying, for helping her children go to college. She earned too much to qualify for financial aid but too little to realistically pay five college tuitions. As the mayor left the event and headed for his car, a Hispanic father fell into his arms and wept as he said something in Spanish. His Star scholar son translated: "My dad says thank you and God bless you, because without you I wouldn't be going to college."

The Star program was a great success right off the bat but did come at a cost, which proved to be quite challenging at a time when the state was failing to fund us fully. But while economic pressures will have to be dealt with on a national basis, free college programs are here to stay and benefit many students who would otherwise never have had the opportunity.

CHAPTER 8

RESULTS–AND RESISTANCE

An Unfinished Journey

Year by year, City Colleges made major strides. By 2016, we were meeting or exceeding most of our academic targets, including graduation rate, certificates awarded, degrees granted, transfer after completion, and transitions from GED and ESL to college credit (see figure 8.1). The graduation rate for first-time, full-time students more than doubled, to 17 percent (and was approaching 18 percent), and for the first time on record, City Colleges granted more than five thousand degrees in a year. The number of degrees awarded was increasing, while the time to completion was decreasing. Overall completion, which counted all students regardless of full-time or part-time status, was up 35 percent. We had saved $70 million through improving our operations. We were exceeding our remediation goal by more than 60 percent. On most other measures, we were within striking distance, and nearly all our goals for 2018 remained within reach.[1]

Our degrees and credentials had proved to be increasingly relevant to employers and universities, and the student learning they symbolized had never held greater promise for our graduates. Not only was the median income of our graduates increasing, but by 2017 we had taken four-year partnerships to a new level.

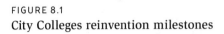

FIGURE 8.1
City Colleges reinvention milestones

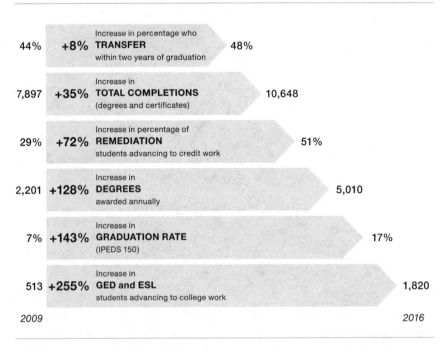

As the results of Reinvention were taking deeper hold within our institution, I got invitations to speak about our reforms to business, education, and government groups across the country. Meeting other community
college presidents and foundation leaders, it was clear to me that we in
Chicago did not have a monopoly on answers and solutions, and we were
not a best-in-class institution. Still, City Colleges was gaining a very good
reputation locally and nationally, given our systemic approach and fast rate
of improvement.

In 2015, one of our colleges, Kennedy-King, was named one of ten final-
ists for the prestigious Aspen Prize for Community College Excellence—a
huge accomplishment for the president, faculty, staff, and administrators
who made this happen. Every other year, the Aspen Institute awards $1
million to community colleges that demonstrate excellence, through quan-
titative and qualitative measures, in completion, learning, labor market

outcomes, and equity. Because of its clear guided pathways, rigorous commitment to student supports, and, most important, tripling of the graduation rate since the launch of Reinvention (although not a factor in the decision this was during a time when 98 percent of its population was in need of remediation), Kennedy-King was the first recipient of Aspen's $100,000 Rising Star award for rapid improvement.

Another, more personal honor occurred later, when the Bill & Melinda Gates Foundation called with an invitation for a one-on-one conversation about community college reform with Bill Gates. In that setting, Gates was sincere and engaging. I have seldom met anyone with more passion for and knowledge about education reform. As a former IT student and professional, meeting Bill Gates was for me like—well, meeting Bill Gates!

Gates decided to highlight my personal and professional story in a video and our work on his blog, where he was kind and generous with his praise:

> Once in a while you meet someone whose work is so extraordinary you want to share their story so others can learn from their experience. That's how I feel about Cheryl Hyman . . . The graduation rate has doubled since 2010 to 14 percent, and for the last three years the school has awarded the highest number of degrees in its history. Much more work, of course, needs to be done. As Cheryl told me, she won't be satisfied until her graduation rate is 100 percent. Still, the progress made by Cheryl is already a reminder that change is possible in higher education. Picking leaders like Chancellor Hyman is a big part of that change. She's setting a fantastic example that more people need to hear about.[2]

This was the praise of a lifetime. It's only human to admit that I was proud of myself and glad my parents were around to see their little girl recognized this way. Mostly, though, I welcomed those words as validation for all our work on behalf of our students, as this was an honor not for *me* but for *everyone at City Colleges*: the presidents leading each college with commitment and skill, the faculty working so hard every day to make that happen and giving so much of their time and valuable thoughts to Reinvention, the administrators working just as hard with little if any recognition, and, most important, the students trying to achieve the same success that I and others had.

● ● ●

While we had plenty to be proud about at City Colleges, we certainly weren't about to hang a "Mission Accomplished" banner. While Reinvention was a quantifiable success overall, there were three areas where we had trouble meeting our targets. The first was adult education. Transitions to college-credit work and level gains were up by almost 300 percent; this was our fourth institutional goal and thus very important to us. But while transitions had more than doubled, we were still missing our annual targets for both GED attainment and for students advancing grade levels. We suspected that part of the reason was the changes Illinois had made in the GED test and the dramatic increase in the cost of taking it, but we could not let that get in the way of progress. We systematically revamped how we taught to better align with the new expectations, but it remains to be seen whether those efforts will pay off.

The second challenge was our adult education enrollment. Early in Reinvention, we had not only rebranded ourselves but launched new marketing highlighting the success of graduates and the real-world relevance of what we taught. As the recession waned and the economy rebounded, more prospective students could go straight into entry-level jobs instead of college if they wanted to. During that time, our GED and ESL enrollment dropped, and our credit enrollment rose only 6 percent—an increase, yes, but one that fell below our target. We suspected that a big reason was that by 2016, in the face of a state budget crisis, Illinois had cut City Colleges funding and stopped supplementing financial aid. This caused the number of City Colleges students eligible for state aid to decline 50 percent, impacting overall credit enrollment.

While much of my team starting focusing on the enrollment data like stockbrokers during a crash, I told them to remain focused on completion. We had moved from an institution that focused only on access—and measured performance simply by counting filled chairs (and the funding that accompanied them)—to one focused on both access and success, and I didn't want our mindset to revert.

In any case, we continued to graduate more students even as our over-all cohort was getting smaller. I was always cognizant of our need to ensure adequate student access.

While of course community colleges that have great outcomes for their students enroll more of them, at the same time they help current students complete and make sure the new students follow in their foot-steps. I believed the best way we could recruit students and ensure we were strategically growing enrollment was to offer high-quality, affordable programs (keeping tuition and fees within the maximum federal Pell grant) that enabled students to complete relevant degrees in as little time as pos-sible. This is not to suggest enrollment doesn't matter, but enrollment just for sake of enrollment can cause one to lose focus on the importance of on-time completion.

The third area in which we fell short of our goals was grants. Both the state and federal government cut back on the kinds of grants that had been our main source of such funding—the federal sequester, which set lower funding levels that remain to this day, meant that grants for everything from job training to tutoring ended up on the chopping block. We worked with businesses and foundations to secure alternative grants to replace those funds. We revamped our foundation so we could, in the future, leverage the expertise and networks of our industry partners by having them more involved on our foundation board and in our fundraising, and we hired new staff to ramp up fundraising now that our outcomes were headed in the right direction and we had a better story to tell.

While the increase in the graduation rate from 7 percent to 17 percent, approaching 18 percent, was a huge accomplishment and secured us the Rising Star distinction from the Aspen Institute, we were still below the national average of 22 percent. Many talk about the 22 percent as if it's something to brag about, and despite our great accomplishment, even I got criticized for not getting our completion rate that high. On the other hand, just before I left office, a leader at City Colleges said to me that because we had reached 17 percent, we "were not in a crisis anymore." I was at a loss for words (and anyone who even half knows me knows that's rare). As I would eventually say in a speech when I left the institution, neither 17 percent nor 22 percent is acceptable, and we all have a long way to go and a lot of work to do. Before Reinvention, our graduation rate had been at the bottom of community college systems in America's largest ten cities (at number 9). We had moved ahead of five cities, but still lagged well behind the three top cities for completion.

• • •

While we leaders have a lot of control over the success of our institutions, our state ecosystems can have a great impact. As much as I refuse to use external factors as an excuse for any way we fell short at City Colleges, any accounting of the challenges of Reinvention—and community colleges in general—must include an understanding of the effect of state policy and funding. My time as a higher education leader gave me insights worth sharing on the policy conditions that can help and hinder colleges as they strive to improve student success.

In 2015, with the General Assembly unable to agree on a state budget for more than two years, Illinois started severely underfunding community colleges, cutting our state allocation in half in addition to reducing state-based financial aid to students in need. While some other states were funding innovations in community colleges—money that could have been used, say, to set up statewide guided pathways—our state wasn't even funding basic needs. (On the financial front, although Illinois reduced its funding, we were more fortunate than our colleagues in Arizona, where the state chose to stop funding community colleges altogether.)

I cannot help but wonder whether states would be less willing to cut community college funding, and whether there would be more pushback when they do cut, if the colleges themselves put more of an emphasis on outcomes and accountability. If people truly understood not just the outcomes but also the impact those outcomes have on our economy, might community colleges receive big endowments the way four-year institutions do? We can all find places to lay blame when educational institutions don't receive the funding they deserve, but as education leaders, we should all consistently ask ourselves what role we play in these dynamics.

I firmly believe that, as much as money matters—for example, since funding was cut, community college graduation rates in Arizona have dropped—more funding is not always the solution to every problem. All the money in the world won't help students if colleges aren't offering them something relevant, operating efficiently, redirecting resources to support them, and tracking progress. By the same token, though, smart approaches to student success can't work if they're not funded. This is why it's immensely important for institutions to have strategic plans with quantifiable measurable goals. Such plans allow those who lead community colleges to better understand what they can and can't do with what they do and don't have. They also allow these institutions to prioritize and make the right trade-offs. In short, money matters. but it can't always be an excuse for poor outcomes and lack of effort.

It won't come as a surprise to learn that I strongly favor performance-based funding, where funds are not allocated merely based on enrollment but also on outcomes like student completion, job placements, and job retention in a student's area of study. Colleges that do better are rewarded for it. But performance funding alone isn't a magic bullet. According to a study by the Community College Research Center at Columbia University, where states added a performance bonus, there was little impact on outcomes; financial incentives, the researchers reported, should be paired with other reforms, and culture and institution-wide tie-ins to the mission are still the key ingredient in bringing about enhanced student success: "If college leaders and faculty do not clearly understand the measures and how they relate to their daily jobs, they are unlikely to embrace them or actively work to improve the institution's performance in term of them."[3]

Tennessee shows how pairing funding and accountability can pay off with strong results. The state committed dollars by repurposing existing funds and adding new funds to provide free associate degrees—that's the access agenda. At the same time, it ties every dollar of state community college funding to outcomes—that's the success agenda. According to the Lumina Foundation, since the reforms, the growth rate of the number of associate degrees awarded each year in Tennessee has doubled.[4] By contrast, when Illinois made a timid foray into outcomes-based funding, it offered a pool of $300,000 for all community colleges in the state combined. Not only is performance-based funding rare, only half of states have put in place rigorous systems to track college student outcomes, according to Complete College America. Not surprisingly, the more successful community colleges tend to be in the states that have done so or have taken steps toward doing so.[5]

At City Colleges, student-success pay—additional payouts to student-facing, unionized employees based on collectively meeting student outcome metrics—was only one way we tried to connect faculty more closely to outcomes. Involving faculty in the task forces and the pathways process allowed us to have a conversation about what successful completion and transfer looks like. Performance pay for faculty and other employees may or may not be the right approach for some institutions, and will continue to be debated for a long time, but the bottom line for me is that institutions need to find a way to hold themselves and each other accountable for low student outcomes, especially when taxpayer dollars are involved.

Additionally, we lack the right policy incentives for student success reform on a national level. There is tremendous opportunity to use local and federal governing bodies to promote polices that will directly improve student success: for example, before approving new programs, local governing agencies could require schools to submit data proving relevance in the labor market or transfer requirements for four-year institutions and the college accreditation process could focus more on outcomes such as completion, job placement and retention, and program relevance. However, these must be developed in concert with each other to maximize their collective impact. Currently, such a comprehensive policy framework does not exist.

All of these factors keep community colleges from reaching their full potential. According to the latest comprehensive data published by the National Center for Education Statistics, the three-year graduation rate for associate degree–seeking students at public community colleges actually decreased from nearly 24 percent in 2000 to just under 22 percent in 2012. Institutional success stories are still the exception rather than the norm.[6]

● ● ●

More than state or federal policy, more than funding, if anything stopped Reinvention from yielding even stronger results, it was our inability to fully change the institutional culture at City Colleges. As we launched Reinvention, we studied a few examples of community colleges that had successfully started on the path to increased completion and relevance, and one stood out dramatically. Valencia College in Orlando, Florida, is a stellar example of what's possible for community colleges, but also an example of what's required: a revolution in institutional culture. That's something we couldn't measure on our scorecard. If we had, we wouldn't have met our goal.

Valencia, the inaugural winner of the Aspen Prize for Community College Excellence, is one of the rare community colleges that has continued to achieve impressive gains and maintain them. Yes, it put into place a host of new systems and supports. But more important, under excellent, long-term leadership, it transformed into an institution where *all* stakeholders put student success at the center of everything they do.[7]

The college has launched initiative after initiative that have resulted in a graduation rate that is well above the national average. Through an unusually collaborative relationship and clear, seamless articulation processes, called DirectConnect, Valencia students have a straight pipeline into the University of Central Florida. An effort called Right Start embeds smart advising and program guidance from the first hours of a student's interaction with the college. Full-time faculty are enrolled in a three-year "learning academy," a professional development incubator where they test out approaches to measure and improve student learning. No student is ever allowed to enroll late in a class that's already met once. Valencia strategically made its five campuses stop competing with each other for students, new programs, and employer partnerships. Every college had its sweet spot. Even more groundbreaking, Valencia did this in concert with other area community colleges.

The *National Journal* has written that it is sometimes hard to tell where the area's colleges ended and the business community started, because the institutions are so embedded. However, Valencia has made sure that programs teach skills that are relevant to industries and not just single employers, to avoid students finding themselves without options if an employer closes shop or leaves town. President Sandy Shugart and his faculty and administrators have created an ecosystem where access and success are interwoven and even interchangeable. As Shugart says: "The trick isn't to get the right learner, the trick is to get the right conditions for that learner."[8]

All of these initiatives work. Valencia has a 44 percent graduation rate, and, remarkably, underrepresented minorities enjoy nearly the same outcomes as everyone else at the college. Shugart, who has led Valencia for

nearly twenty years, didn't just change programs and processes at Valencia. He changed the priorities. He started by asking two simple questions:
"Are students learning?" and "How do we know?" The answers inform
every choice made throughout the college. Shugart was so intent in changing the mindset from just enrollment to outcomes that he famously stopped
distribution of enrollment reports to faculty.[9]

• • •

But would these initiatives work so well if they were merely plopped into
another college? Probably not. When he discusses how his institution
achieved this success, Shugart doesn't dwell on policy or programs. He
talks about the culture. City Colleges certainly achieved a lot over a short
few years. Reinvention definitely challenged, and changed, some long-held
attitudes that served those who worked there more than those who studied
there. But I know today, to a much greater extent than I did when I was
appointed, that changing culture is a lengthy process—much longer then
my tenure.

It was the proverbial one step forward, two steps back, even as we won
awards, even as I was asked to present our successes at conferences, even
as more and more students graduated each year. I was invited to meet one
on one with one of the most powerful philanthropists on Earth so he could
learn what we were doing, but some of the folks at home, especially on our
campuses, had a whole different kind of meeting in store for me.

In 2015, more than five years into my tenure, I began to get reports
from my senior staff that faculty (some of the same individuals who had
served on the original reinvention task forces) opposed to Reinvention
were organizing a of vote no confidence in my leadership. In the proposed
resolution, these detractors said they sought "a Chancellor who is responsive to student and faculty concerns, demonstrates a commitment to the
[City Colleges of Chicago] mission, respects shared governance, and comes
from an educational background."

In the face of resistance, leaders can sometimes lose their connection
with their goals and with the institution they lead. Perhaps this had happened to me. I once understood why people were resisting Reinvention,
even though I didn't always think there was a need to. But by this point

I just didn't understand the opposition anymore—the fight seem to be so much bigger than the changes themselves.

From my team's perspective, everyone seemed to be winning. Students were learning, graduating on time, and getting jobs in their area of study. Faculty were able to continue teaching as they always had, and hadn't lost their jobs even when the institution's funding was weakened. Regional employers and four-year colleges finally believed that City Colleges graduates were worth recruiting. National and international publications took notice of College to Careers and Reinvention as a model to follow. So what were the real problems?

That year, the head of the Faculty Council had told our board of directors in a public meeting that City Colleges had violated the terms of its Higher Learning Commission accreditation. The council argued that our academic decisions were "not legitimate" and that "Reinvention initiatives are not in the best interest of our students or our mission, and many District Office decisions are diverting the City Colleges from their primary responsibility to provide education and promote the public good." Furthermore, "District Office plans to eliminate or consolidate the vast majority of City Colleges' academic programs and to prioritize job training." Although the Higher Learning Commission would find these claims to be wholly unsubstantiated, it was certainly a problem that this was how our leadership was perceived.

According to the proposed resolution, I had failed "to provide sufficient rationale for [my] policies, especially the consolidation of programs." We had carefully structured the program consolidations tied to College to Careers to build pathways for great careers in all parts of the city. Even though specific programs were based on specific campuses, we still offered many career-focused courses in this area and others (including general education) on multiple campuses and had even agreed to push back our timelines to give those affected more time to prepare. Additionally, in areas where we found it was better to build bridges rather than a complete consolidation, we did so; for example, in our TDL program at Kennedy- King College, in addition to being focused on the culinary and hospitality industries, we had a state-of-the-art automotive facility built as part of the school prior to my tenure. We maintained that presence because of the major capital investment instead of trying to move these programs from

Kennedy-King to Olive-Harvey, our TDL College to Careers center of excellence. The same was true for our manufacturing programs. Wright College, home to our IT College to Careers center of excellence, had a previously existing manufacturing program with some minor capital investments, so we built bridges between that program and our programs at Daley College, the center of excellence for manufacturing.

Still, some critics believed that consolidation discriminated against students based on geography—that it furthered segregation to center specific programs on specific campuses. Even though from my vantage point we were prioritizing quality over convenience and were vastly improving opportunities for students, some students said at board meetings that they were being done a disservice. Opposition is to be expected when driving large-scale, change, but hearing students express these feelings was the hardest part for me. Knowing their struggles firsthand, I understood their perspective very well, but I also knew the sacrifices one must make to rise out of poverty in society (and today's society is far more competitive). I also knew what it is like to work hard in school, anticipating that the hard work will pay off with meaningful credentials, only to learn that this is not be the case. I had had no other reason to accept the position as chancellor than helping city college's students, so I was most affected by their critiques.

By now, in the final stages of consolidating our College to Careers programs, one program consolidation was drawing far more pronounced and persistent opposition than others. Students, community groups, elected officials, and faculty all voiced concerns about the program not being located on multiple campuses. They weren't swayed by the fact we were planning a million-dollar investment in a state-of-the-art lab—which was too expensive to replicate across campuses even if we thought that was a good idea. My senior leadership team, and sometimes I, met with each group of opponents several times and presented our case in public hearings and offered compromises. But nothing would persuade the most radical and vocal opponents to consider compromises (which may have at times polarized others who might have been more willing to compromise), even though by now successes stemming from programs such as Healthcare, TDL and Business were already seeing positive tangible results..

Some dissatisfied faculty members believed I had no respect for general academics—that I wanted to push out traditional subjects like English and history in favor of more specifically career-focused classes. They saw this in the creation of College to Careers, and in what they said was the elimination of "the entire academic affairs department." We had in fact merged the academic affairs and the Reinvention departments into one office of strategy and academic governance, led by Rasmus Lynnerup, while each college maintained its own academic affairs leadership in the form of vice presidents and deans of instruction. We didn't do this to eliminate or reduce the importance of academic affairs, but to better advance it by ensuring the best possible coordination. The new structure, I thought, allowed for greater consultation about academic policies and impacts with the experts in academic affairs as we further developed, structured and implemented our reforms while closely monitoring our goals and outcomes.

Another bone of contention was whether a PhD should be a required credential for the individual leading the new department of strategy and academic governance. While most of our college presidents, top administrators in academic-related posts, and the person who led academic policy and compliance matters for City Colleges in the new department had PhDs, not all did, which drew consistent criticism. This was ironic, since many of these opponents were among the several faculty members who, in partnership with the Faculty Council, had overhauled all aspects of faculty credentialing, tenure, and development.

In addition to the PhD question, there was contention because Rasmus's title was "Executive Vice Chancellor of Strategy and Academic Governance" rather than "Provost." To me, this argument signaled that much of the opposition grew out discomfort with change, focusing on old habits rather than being open to the function and services the new structure was providing.

The resolution also protested our tuition increases and the earlier course registration deadline—two changes that critics said were negatively affecting student access, even though our research showed otherwise. Again, this was a reversal: both faculty and students had regularly complained about late registration in our early briefings—faculty were upset that allowing students to register on the last day before classes started, or even later, did not give them or students time to prepare or purchase books, and students complained about lack of availability with classes and books and having time to prepare.

Finally, the proposed no-confidence resolution charged that I was not "sufficiently engaged with students and faculty." That there was not enough consultation with the administration was a recurring theme in grievances from faculty and some community groups. They said they didn't oppose change, but they craved more communication and clarity.

This was hard for me to understand. In the ways I thought mattered most, I was very engaged, and we had built many channels of communication. These included regular discipline meetings, biweekly meetings with college presidents, the Reinvention task force team member meetings, monthly meetings with the Faculty Council and my senior leadership team to discuss their issues and concerns. The City Colleges also had a government and community relations team that frequently meet with community groups and elected officials. In addition to all the regular meetings my staff conducted with leaders throughout the colleges, I met with the student government association and held meetings with groups of students at each college annually. At annual meetings at the seven colleges, I sought feedback from faculty and students in honest conversations. In the original phases of Reinvention, I visited the task forces at least daily.

But it is true that, as time went by, I had less face time with students and faculty. In part, this was a deliberate strategy. Once the task forces transitioned into the colleges, I stepped back so that the college presidents would be perceived, rightfully, as the leaders of what happened on their campuses. While I continued to hold biweekly full-day meetings with the presidents, I thought that spending too much time on campuses would draw me into day-to-day issues when I needed to be focused on the bigger picture. I never denied a meeting request from any elected official, I responded to every email and phone call, and I had a web link established called "Ask the Chancellor." When it came to being present, I thought I was striking the right balance.

Others clearly thought otherwise. And by the end, I *had* retreated somewhat. Given the acrimony swirling around me and my team, I felt like my presence would be a distraction for those working to ensure progress continued.

One additional point of controversy arose because, at the request of families and others in the City Colleges community, we had awarded six posthumous honorary degrees to qualified students whose lives were cut short just before they were scheduled to graduate. The families who accepted these honors on behalf of their loved ones expressed tremendous gratitude. Because they were honorary, we didn't count any of the credentials toward our graduation rate. Yet sadly and predictably, a local media outlet falsely reported that City Colleges was "inflating" its completion numbers by graduating students who had passed away before actually completing.[10] Soon another ran with it, without contacting us, then another. This wasn't the first time and wouldn't be the last that criticism divorced from facts had journeyed outside our walls, but this time it impugned my and my team's integrity.

The no-confidence resolution certainly didn't reflect the views of all professors. I believe some Faculty Council officers at the district level didn't agree, and some faculty at the campuses were concerned that the vote had not been democratic and violated the Faculty Council constitution. In the end, the resolution, which declared that the council had "no confidence in Chancellor Hyman's ability to govern the City Colleges of Chicago," was passed at only two of the seven colleges.

Point by point, I felt that the criticisms didn't add up, though they weren't news to me. By this time, and well before the vote took place, I had told my kitchen cabinet that I thought the time had come for me to leave City Colleges. I had resisted that conclusion for a long time. Reinvention was about upsetting the apple cart, so I always knew friction and even rejection were part of the package—these are a given when attempting to change culture. What some saw as sharpness I saw as passion, what some saw as toughness I saw as bluntness. Sadly, I'm not sure this assessment was always divorced from my gender. In male executives, would these same character traits be more easily accepted?

So I asked myself, *Why are you quitting on this unfinished job? Why are you quitting on these students?* We were accomplishing so much, and had a chance to reach the national average graduation rate. There was a year left in our five-year plan.

But even if you know your cause is just, there comes a time when you can't face the resistance alone. During my last year, I had to accept the reality that politics often trumps performance. No person or institution operates in a vacuum; politics always finds its way into academia—especially public institutions—for better or worse. I had come to believe, or at least hope, that the energy that was being expended on opposing me and opposing Reinvention might be redirected toward helping students. Even though the fight should have never been about me, that's what it had become. Without me, the institution could be free, in a way, to write its next chapter.

CHAPTER 9

REFLECTIONS

The Twenty-Four-Block Journey

When college and civic leaders pull me aside at national gatherings, they do not ask me about City Colleges' academic model, the fiscal reforms, or how we partnered with industry as much as they ask me this: How do you make the cultural changes that make all the other changes possible? It's the right question. And the fact that I left without my agenda fully completed shows it's one I was never able to fully answer.

One of the greatest challenges for those charged with reforming community colleges is how they can move their institutions to embrace a culture that is totally and strategically focused on student success, a culture that's based in an accountability system where their experience and expertise is guided by data on outcomes—regardless of pushback, regardless of the cost to us as leaders. Creating an environment that prioritizes student outcomes and the strategies necessary to achieve them requires navigating over innumerable choppy waves, commanding a crew sometimes unfamiliar with the waters. There are barely visible barriers, lurking icebergs.

One of the most significant barriers is the concept of shared governance—or at least the concept as some perceive it. The no-confidence resolution drawn up against me declared that the "corporate governance model in place at District Office is antithetical to the ideals of *shared* governance essential to fulfilling our educational responsibilities." *Shared governance* is a vague term that means different things to different people.[1] To many in higher education, including me, it means that constituents get to participate at different points in the decision-making process; their input is sought and they're kept informed. To the faculty who continually opposed Reinvention, though, it felt to me that it was not about sharing at all, but rather that administrators were supposed to have very limited input on all things academic, whereas faculty would have a say on all administrative matters. Of course, that's unrealistic: such an arrangement would fail to provide the balance or benefits the institution needed to achieve sustainable change.

Looking back, I ask myself if we could have taken Reinvention further if I had done some things differently. The answer is, maybe. I could have taken more time to seek consensus and build buy-in for our initiatives. I could have had more meetings at the colleges, so I wouldn't have given the impression I was detached. I could also have met more often with elected officials and community activists, to keep them engaged when they felt that they weren't. Perhaps that would have avoided some friction and maybe even spared me the no-confidence resolution. As I write this book and look back over my seven years as chancellor, I see that there may indeed have been opportunities to go along a different path. I believe I am opened-minded enough to understand different approaches may lead to a different result.

But in the end, it seems to me that the issue was never really about the quality or quantity of the communications, but the very essence of what was being communicated. I'm not sure there was any way I could have engaged people to get them on board with a wholesale change in how City Colleges approached student success. I'm not sure I could have ever gotten them to embrace the perceived radical reforms needed to meaningfully improve students' higher education outcomes.

Collaboration does not always equal consensus, and decision making by leaders does not always equal autocracy. I believed then, as I do now, that it was my job to exercise my best judgment to achieve the best results for the students of City Colleges of Chicago and the institution itself, and that's what I did. A rapid pace was important not just in practical terms but so that people could see and feel success, which fuels more success. For example, members of the eight task forces were able to watch their recommendations turn into policy and practice—and result in a rapid burst of positive outcomes for students. They felt ownership in the changes, felt their ideas and suggestions were being heard. They could see what they suggested come to fruition, and they knew outsiders were seeing the progress as well.

Yet even the consensus built into the task force process may have hindered progress. If the private sector took initiative at the plodding pace of proponents of universal shared decision making, imagine how slow corporations would be to launch products, advance technology, and meet market needs. Rapid best practice adoption is one of the things *Fortune* 500 companies do best, and it is paramount that community college systems move fast too—the clock is ticking. While we secure consensus on everything, students suffer.

How much progress would we have sacrificed if we had moved more slowly, or made more compromises? Our rapidly increasing graduation rate meant that thousands more students earned credentials than would have without Reinvention. How many of those credentials would we have sacrificed?

Criticism often centered on bringing in "outsiders" to City Colleges— starting with me. I, of course, had no professional background in academia; I hired people who had worked as higher education administrators alongside leading strategy consultants from the likes of McKinsey and Accenture—people driven to move from profit-making companies to something more personally meaningful, even if it meant a pay cut. Community colleges must redefine talent and align their practices with the outside world. Chancellors and presidents in big-city environments especially have a diverse pool of talent to draw from. We must be open to and invite outside professionals with different academic and career paths who can broaden perspectives and enable new approaches to bring about dramatic change. People within academia can't be so afraid of a so-called "corporate takeover of education." Instead they should be embracing the integration of business insights and skills coupled with the expertise of highly dedicated educators that can help us bring relevance to our programs and run our institutions more efficiently. Educational boards, too, might benefit by emulating corporate boards in expecting and demanding results. They should put more focus on student outcomes and operational excellence and hold leaders and those who work for them accountable for those outcomes.

At City Colleges, resistance to businesspeople and a business mindset helped prevent us from ever fully changing the culture of the institution, and thus from ensuring that our work reached its fullest potential for students. But even though there were tactical and implementation approaches that we could have thought through better, and we could have made some choices that better accommodated political realities, in terms of the big-picture elements and initiatives of Reinvention, there's little I would change. If anything, I would have tried to make them happen faster, because the ultimate lesson is that sometimes our window to act is short.

While the details differ across states and colleges, this is a challenge for all higher education leaders. We need agents of change in leadership positions, not administrators who know there are failures in the system but are loath to or unable to disrupt the status quo. Those selecting tomorrow's college leaders shouldn't just look for candidates with only education backgrounds, they should also insist on candidates with a willingness to run toward the fight, who also come with built-in flak jackets that will protect them from all the incoming rounds related to reform and transformation.

It is all too easy to succumb to the path of least resistance, to replay the few success stories while ignoring the many other ways progress has stagnated. Even the best leaders sometimes make mistakes—that's the price of taking chances. Worse than taking risks that don't pan out is not taking risks at all, hesitating out of fear of criticism and retaliation.

● ● ●

To be an effective leader, you have to be willing to walk away at any time. From my first day as chancellor, I believed that if you prize your title or stature or salary a little too much, you might make compromises that lengthen your tenure but hinder your ability to fulfill your mission. So it was that in the spring of 2016, I announced my decision to only renew my contract for a year, to use that year to allow for a smooth transition to new leadership.

The most frequent question I got after the announcement was, "What are you going to do next?" My answer was, "I am going to sleep for eight hours straight at least once. I am going to disconnect my phone, and I am going to finally take a vacation." I wasn't joking. I needed to make sure I allowed myself the time to reenergize, so that whatever my next journey was, I could pursue it with the same passion and fire I had when I'd started this one.

I had been chancellor at City Colleges for seven years, longer than the average tenure for community college presidents. Still, I was leaving with business unfinished. There were several areas that, with hindsight, I wish we would have developed more. For one, while Reinvention had a huge impact, we could have achieved more if we had trained employees more systematically. At every turn, every implementation, we should have had more consistently insisted on answering two questions: "Do all employees know about this? Have we given them the tools to share this with students effectively?" We did develop a handbook and a "train the trainer" process, but there often was a gap between when we made changes and when advisers, admissions specialists, recruiters, and faculty were equipped to explain them to students. That meant that students weren't always as informed as possible at critical goal-setting moments, and implementation wasn't as consistent as it could have been.

I also wish we would have further fleshed out predictive scheduling. I would have liked us to build course schedules based on students' time preferences and demands. Even more, my dream was for City Colleges students to be able to know their two-year schedule on day one and have the ability to choose whole-cohort enrollment, where they would be grouped with students with similar academic goals and proceed through their program together, as I did in my executive MBA program. If students could attend at a set and compact time—say, every Tuesday and Thursday morning for two years—it would be easier to organize their professional and personal lives around their academic ones.

I wish we had built new performance reviews for administrators and expanded accountability on an individual level for some groups of employees and for faculty collectively. Finally, I wish I had done more to scale to all seven colleges the remediation and the new student experience changes we started at Wright College.

These are tactical changes, though. The more important changes for community colleges across the country are radical. Put simply, we must fundamentally redefine quality. All that matters is that many more students complete *relevant* credentials. The national completion agenda is a step in the right direction, but it can't end there. Just as enrollment cannot be a goal unto itself, neither can completion. A certificate or degree that does not ultimately stack into a larger degree or certificate, that does not both transfer to a four-year university and lead to career growth, gives students short-term success with no long-term value. Only by judging community college outcomes in the harshest light—*Does this position graduates for a lifetime of success?*—can we redeem decades of abominable performance. In my seven years there, City Colleges nearly tripled its graduation rate and more than doubled the number of degrees awarded, even when enrollment fluctuated. And it was not enough.

The funding and accreditation processes must be centered on a new definition of relevant completion, so that we have more built-in demands related to the kind of quality that truly matters. And a new, courageous cadre of community college leaders must embrace this goal and the intersecting access and success measures it comprises.

They must do so urgently. College presidents—particularly those at community colleges—do not have much time. People talk about change taking years or even decades, but leadership retention numbers demand a different theory of change. I helmed the ship for longer than average and still did not witness the conclusion of my own official five-year plan.

Still, I can say with pride and confidence that thanks to the hard work of many stakeholders, City Colleges absolutely improved during my tenure. Thousands of students gained relevant credentials who wouldn't have otherwise done so. Even at the board of trustees meeting when the no-confidence vote was announced, I was fortunate to hear partners and friends and students from many years of Reinvention affirm this.

I was touched by the testimony of US Representative Bobby Rush, who left his ailing wife's hospital room to attend the meeting. The congressman told the standing-room-only audience:

> Reinvention is far more difficult than recycling. There are some who want us to recycle personalities. They don't want change. They fight change with everything that they have, because change is threatening to their sense of being comfortable, to their predictive futures. Cheryl shakes that comfort zone . . . That she has raised the graduation rate in this city is phenomenal.

Larry Goodman, the head of Rush University Medical Center, said:

What was impressive to me, as I got to know the chancellor, was that these things are not simple . . . What I was particularly impressed with was, frankly, the pace of change and how effective it was. In the end, Rush is focused on trying to address, in our community, health-care inequities. We look for strong partners that are equally committed, and there's no question City Colleges, with this board and the leadership of Chancellor Hyman, is a partner that we are pleased to work with.

After the meeting, those leading the vote marched to City Hall to deliver the resolution to the Office of the Mayor. Mayor Emanuel was not there, but his press team was, and they delivered this statement:

Under Cheryl's leadership, the City Colleges of Chicago has more than doubled its graduation rate, while making significant invest-ments to improve student outcomes. Today, not only are more stu-dents graduating than ever before, but they are graduating from programs that have been validated by both employers and four-year universities. The mayor is committed to working with the chancel-lor as CCC continues to provide an affordable pathway to a four-year degree while also expanding industry-aligned opportunities that provide great value to both our students, as well as to top employers seeking highly qualified candidates for the jobs of today.

When I announced my departure, a headline ran in Chicago media that my tenure had been stormy.[2] Very true indeed. You do not change the status quo *without* some storms. The more you demand in terms of results and accountability, the bigger the storms. I was shocked by how personal and offensive the opposition had become, and yet it was important in my last year at City Colleges to not get cynical. Cynicism can be provocative and can even be an effective trait for those resisting change, but it is dan-gerous and it can lead people and institutions astray—it requires a basic loss of faith in people and the ability of a team to get things done.

I remain honored and grateful to have led the institution that gave me my start in life, and even more thankful to those who allowed me the opportunity and those who supported me along the way. My goal was always to realize its mission of student success—to play a role in giving others a chance to have successful starts too.

You cannot quantify values. No matter our differences, every member of the faculty, staff, and leadership at the City Colleges of Chicago shared the value that all residents of the city, regardless of background or need, deserve a chance, and a second chance, and a third chance to use education to build—and to rebuild—their lives. There was no number that quantified that burning desire we shared, one that had burned in me since I began building my own life at Olive-Harvey, one that burned in professors and others who met day in and day out with students who had backgrounds similar to mine. We all made it our mission to have students define and achieve their dreams.

Whether my opponents were right or whether I was—or whether we both were—will be determined over time and is for others to judge. For me, the no-confidence resolution simply meant that we had taken the risk on hard fights to raise student achievement at City Colleges. That vote turned out to be the necessary price of giving more students a shot at graduating with a credential that opens the door to a good career and life.

A leader and an institution can only create the conditions for change to be sustainable, but *sustainable* is not a synonym for *eternal*. Some of the changes we instituted over seven years could, and perhaps will, be erased in an instant. Others—student pathways and degree audit technology and processes, capital investments, some performance management principles—would be harder to undo. But no matter what new and future leaders decide about specific tactics, we know that we instilled a new sense of hope in many at City Colleges, a new appreciation of the importance of accountability and relevant credentials, and a new understanding of what's possible for students. Partnerships can dissolve, accountability systems can deteriorate, but the drive for results becomes a habit hard to kick.

● ● ●

Education is one of the leading civil rights issues in our time and racial gaps in education attainment are not closing. The graduation rate is 43 percent for whites but only 21 percent for blacks and 16 percent for Hispanics. This is unconscionable.[3] When community college stakeholders make too many compromises and skirt the big reforms required, it is the students whose time is wasted and who foot a hefty bill. If community colleges are to live up to their mission and their public obligation, they must promote credentials of social and economic value. Community colleges must close equity gaps, giving more advantages to people who have fewer advantages. Programmatically, this is a perennial academic alignment and realignment proposition that shifts with the political climate. Whether and how to tighten that alignment, and keep it tight, was the philosophical center of Reinvention.

My journey from a young girl who once dropped out of high school to the leader of the massive institution that once gave her back her start in life consisted of just twenty-four blocks: the length of pavement from the Henry Horner housing projects to the downtown headquarters of the City Colleges of Chicago. Twenty-four blocks is a short distance, yet all my obstacles in life made the destination feel so out of reach. I had walked those twenty-four blocks in our students' shoes, and that sharpened my vision and daily purpose as chancellor.

Students see college as a ticket to a career. They know that you cannot pursue life's loftier goals if you cannot feed yourself and take care of your family. That was a lesson I learned along my twenty-four-block journey and one that is often overlooked. Rather than having false debates wrapped in buzzwords and jargon, we should simply measure our success by whether students are leaving our institutions as productive citizens entering good careers, and whether we've prepared them well for that.

The debate continues.

NOTES

CHAPTER 1

1. Scott A. Ginder et. al., *Enrollment and Employees in Postsecondary Institutions, Fall 2015,* (Washington, DC: National Center for Education Statistics, February 2017.

2. National Center for Education Statistics, "Percentage of 18- to 24-Year-Olds Enrolled in Degree-Granting Postsecondary Institutions, by Level of Institution and Sex and Race/Ethnicity of Student: 1970 through 2015," https://nces.ed.gov/programs/digest/d16/tables/dt16_302.60.asp.

3. City Colleges of Chicago, "Reinvention, Chapter 1" Spring 2011, https://www.ccc.edu/menu/Documents/Reinvention/REI_Reinvention_Chapter_1_03302011.pdf, 43; City Colleges of Chicago, "Five-Year Plan: Strategic Initiatives and Objectives, 2013–2018," http://www.ccc.edu/Documents/strategic%20initiatives_3%2020%2014.pdf.

4. "Reinvention, Chapter 1," 12, 20.

5. Civic Consulting Alliance, "City Colleges of Chicago: Promises and Possibilities," unreleased draft for discussion, 2007, 5, 7.

6. Interview with Brian Fabes, September 26, 2016.

7. "Reinvention, Chapter 1.

8. Adam Walinsky, "What It's Like to Be in Hell," *New York Times,* December 4, 1987.

9. Kenneth Meier, *The Community College Mission: History and Theory, 1930–2000* (PhD thesis, The University of Arizona, 2008), 16. Until very recently, the scholarship on community colleges was long on history and theory and short on data-driven assessment of results. Much of it remains so. Arthur Cohen and Florence Drawer's *The American Community College* (most recent is 6th ed. [San Francisco: Jossey-Bass, 2014]) is widely considered as an unavoidable work on the topic. Cohen and Brawer prefer to focus on the non-measurable contributions of community colleges: "It is easy to reduce the institution's value to the increase in its graduates' social mobility and to ignore its position as a center of acculturation and historical continuity." First published in 1981, it was not until later editions in the 2000s that the book included some still scant data on and examples of community colleges outcomes.

10. Meier, *The Community College Mission,* 299.

CHAPTER 2

1. Much of the history in this section comes from Steven Brint and Jerome Karabel, *The Diverted Dream: Community Colleges and the Promise of Educational Opportunity in America, 1900–1985* (New York: Oxford University Press, 1989).

2. Ibid., 23–26.

3. Elbert K. Fretwell Jr., *Founding Public Junior Colleges: Local Initiative in Six Communities* (New York: Columbia University, 1954), 21–23.

4. Brint and Karabel, *Diverted Dream*, 69–70.

5. The White House Office of the Press Secretary, "Excerpts of the President's remarks in Warren, Michigan and Fact Sheet on the American Graduation Initiative" July 14, 2009, https://www.whitehouse.gov/the-press-office/excerpts-presidents-remarks-warren-michigan-and-fact-sheet-american-graduation-init.

6. Jason Amos, "Preparing the Workers of Today for the Jobs of Tomorrow," *Straight A's: Public Education Policy and Progress* 9, no. 15 (July 2009), http://all4ed.org/articles/preparing-the-workers-of-today-for-the-jobs-of-tomorrow-president-obamas-council-of-economic-advisers-finds-occupations-requiring-higher-education-will-grow-faster-than-occupations-that-do-n/.

7. Lumina Foundation for Education, *A Stronger Nation Through Education: How and Why Americans Must Meet a "Big Goal" for College Attainment*, special report, February 2009, 2–3, 37–38.

8. Ibid.

9. Anthony P. Carnevale, Nicole Smith, and Jeff Strohe, *Help Wanted: Projections of Jobs and Education Requirements Through 2018*, executive Summary (Washington, DC: The Georgetown University Center on Education and the Workforce, June 2010).

10. Elizabeth Z. Rutschow, et al., *Turning the Tide: Five Years of Achieving the Dream in Community Colleges* (New York: MDRC and Community College Research Center, February 2011).

11. The White House Summit on Community Colleges, *Summit Report*, June 2011, https://obamawhitehouse.archives.gov/sites/default/files/uploads/community_college_summit_report.pdf.

12. City Colleges of Chicago, ""Reinvention, Chapter 1," 2011, https://www.ccc.edu/menu/Documents/Reinvention/REI_Reinvention_Chapter_1_03302011.pdf, 21, 38.

13. "Expose of the Manipulation of Data Used to Justify the Reinvention," *City Colleges of Chicago Reinvention: The Truth* (blog), April 28, 2011, http://citycollegeschicagoreinvention-truths.blogspot.com/2011/04/expose-of-manipulation-of-data-used-to.html#comment-form.

14. Sheldon Liebman, "The Case for Change: Reinventing the Wheel at the City Colleges of Chicago," American Association of University Professors, Fall 2011 Academe web posting, www.ilaauo.org/Fall2011k.pdf; *Longitudinal Outcomes*

for New College Credit Students: A Six-Year Tracking Report for Students at the City Colleges of Chicago," City Colleges of Chicago Office of Research and Evaluation internal report, September 2007.

15. *Community College FAQs*, Community College Research Center at Teachers College, Columbia University, http://ccrc.tc.columbia.edu/Community-College-FAQs.html: and Elizabeth Noll et al., *College Students with Children: National and Regional Profiles* (Washington, DC: Student Success Parent Initiative, Institute for Women's Policy Research, January 2017.

16. City Colleges of Chicago, "Reinvention, Chapter 1," 11.

17. "Data Fest," *Harold Lounge* (blog), March 19, 2011, https://haroldlounge.com/2011/03/page/8/.

CHAPTER 3

1. *City Colleges of Chicago: Vision 2011*, internal document.

2. These include the report of the White House Summit on Community Colleges (published in 2011); Complete College America, *Time Is the Enemy* (Fall 2011), https://www.luminafoundation.org/files/resources/time-is-the-enemy.pdf; Joshua S. Wyner, *What Excellent Community Colleges Do: Preparing All Students for Success* (Cambridge, MA: Harvard Educational Publishing Group, 2014); and Thomas R. Bailey, Shanna Smith Jaggars, and Davis Jenkins, *Redesigning America's Community Colleges* (Cambridge, MA: Harvard University Press, 2015).

3. Not surprisingly, in 2011 Valencia would become the inaugural winner of the Aspen Prize for Community College Excellence, which awards $1 million to institutions with strong records in completion, equity, and labor market outcomes.

4. City Colleges of Chicago, "Reinvention, Chapter 1," 2011, https://www.ccc.edu/menu/Documents/Reinvention/REI_Reinvention_Chapter_1_03302011.pdf, 30–31; City Colleges of Chicago, *Spring 2011 Task Force Recommendations*, internal document, 5.

5. City Colleges of Chicago, "Reinvention, Chapter 2: Foundation for Success, 2012,7–8,http://www.ccc.edu/menu/Documents/Reinvention/Reinvention%20 chap%202%20FOR%20WEB.pdf.

6. "Reinvention, Chapter 2," 6.

7. City Colleges of Chicago internal survey, https://www.surveymonkey.com/sr .aspx?sm = us9MTWJEMIJJvSDUvZWeIkWCL5Z39d1yMW1J0T34BYU_3d.

8. Ibid.

9. "ReinQuestion? Vol. 14," *Harold Lounge* (blog), April 7, 2011, https://harold lounge.com/2011/04/07/reinquestion-vol-14/.

10. Ibid.

11. Yami Guzman, "Success from the Inside," *Talk 2 Us COE* (Reinvention team blog),

December 9, 2011, https://talk2uscoe.wordpress.com/2011/12/09/success-from-the-inside/.

12. Deanna Isaacs, "The 7 Percent Solution," *Chicago Reader*, August 4, 2011.

CHAPTER 4

1. Fran Spielman, "City Colleges Cutting Staff, Costs to Focus on Students," *Chicago Sun-Times*, July 30, 2010; John Byrne, "City Colleges Plan to Lay Off 225," *Chicago Tribune*, July 29, 2010.

2. Rhea Kelly, "Campus Technology Announces 2014 Innovators Award Honorees," *Campus Technology,* June 3, 2014.

CHAPTER 5

1. David Goldfield, ed., *Encyclopedia of American History*, vol. 1 (Thousand Oaks, CA: Sage, 2007), 331.

2. Steven Brint and Jerome Karabel, *The Diverted Dream: Community Colleges and the Promise of Educational Opportunity in America, 1900–1985* (New York: Oxford University Press, 1989), 36, 45.

3. Ibid., 54–56.

4. https://nces.ed.gov/pubs2010/2010167.pdf.

5. Kevin Egan et al., *The American Freshman: Fifty-Year Trends, 1966–2016* (Los Angeles: Higher Education Research Institute at UCLA), 2016.

6. Elbert K. Fretwell Jr., *Founding Public Junior Colleges: Local Initiative in Six Communities* (New York: Columbia University, 1954), 41.

7. Monique Garcia, "Simon Calls for Improving Community College Graduation Rate," *Chicago Tribune*, January 18, 2012, http://articles.chicagotribune.com/2012-01-18/news/ct-met-sheila-simon-community-colleges-20120119_1_city-colleges-remedial-courses-student-success-rates.

8. United States Senate Health, Education, Labor and Pensions Committee, *For Profit Higher Education: The Failure to Safeguard the Federal Investment and Ensure Student Success*, majority committee staff report and accompanying minority committee staff views (July 30, 2012), 2–3, https://www.help.senate.gov/imo/media/for_profit_report/PartI-PartIII-SelectedAppendixes.pdf.

9. Joshua S. Wyner, *What Excellent Community Colleges Do: Preparing All Students for Success* (Cambridge: Harvard Educational Publishing Group, 2014), 102.

10. Heart Research Associates, *Falling Short? College Learning and Career Success: Selected Findings from Online Surveys of Employers and College Students Conducted on Behalf of the Association of American Colleges & Universities* (Washington, DC: Heart Research Associates, January 2015), 10, 12, https://www.aacu.org/sites/default/files/files/LEAP/2015employerstudentsurvey.pdf.

11. Brint and Karabel, *The Diverted Dream*, v.

12. http://nursing.illinois.gov/PDF/IlApNursingEdProgPassRates.PDF.

13. Rahm Emanuel speech, December 11, 2011, ttps://www.cityofchicago.org/content/dam/city/depts/mayor/Press%20Room/Press%20Releases/2011/December/12.12.11College2CareersSpeech.pdf.

CHAPTER 6

1. City Colleges of Chicago, *Case for Change* (internal report, October 2010) 20–21.
2. Complete College America, *Time Is the Enemy*. 2011, http://completecollege.org/docs/Time_Is_the_Enemy.pdf.
3. Thomas R. Bailey, Shanna Smith Jaggars, and Davis Jenkins, *Redesigning America's Community Colleges: A Clearer Path to Student Success* (Cambridge, MA: Harvard University Press, 2014), 23, 202–205, 206–210.
4. http://highered.aspeninstitute.org/aspen-prize-program/lake-area-technical-institute/; https://www.lakeareatech.edu/outcomes/; Joshua S. Wyner, *What Excellent Community Colleges Do: Preparing All Students for Success* (Cambridge: Harvard Educational Publishing Group, 2014), 15–18.
5. Wyner, *What Excellent Community Colleges Do*, 24; https://guttman.cuny.edu/about/fast-facts/.
6. *Project Win-Win at the Finish Line* (Washington, DC: Institute for Higher Education Policy, October 2013), http://www.ihep.org/research/publications/project-win-win-finish-line.
7. In fact, retroactive degrees didn't fundamentally change our success equation. Over five years, they made up less than 10 percent of all degrees granted. Ninety-five percent of retroactive degrees go to students who completed their coursework at City Colleges in the four years preceding their receiving their degree. City Colleges awarded only fifty-three reverse-transfer degrees out of nearly nineteen thousand degrees over last five years, though the goal is to significantly grow that number in coming years in partnership with four-year universities.
8. Anthony Carnevale et al., *The College Payoff: Education, Occupations, Lifetime Earnings*, p. 2, https://cew.georgetown.edu/wp-content/uploads/2014/11/collegepayoff-summary.pdf, retrieved June 13, 2017.

CHAPTER 7

1. Thomas Bailey, Dong Wook Jeong, and Sung-Woo Cho, *Referral, Enrollment, and Completion in Developmental Education Sequences in Community Colleges* (New York: Columbia University Community College Research Center Teachers College, Columbia University, November 2009), 3.
2. City Colleges of Chicago, "Reinvention, Chapter 1," 2011https://www.ccc.edu/menu/Documents/Reinvention/REI_Reinvention_Chapter_1_03302011.pdf, 19, 24.
3. Rahm Emanuel speech, December 11, 2011, ttps://www.cityofchicago.org/content/dam/city/depts/mayor/Press%20Room/Press%20Releases/2011/December/12.12.11College2CareersSpeech.pdf.

CHAPTER 8

1. City Colleges of Chicago, "Five-Year Plan: Strategic Initiatives and Objectives, 2013–2018," http://www.ccc.edu/Documents/strategic%20initiatives_3%2020 %2014.pdf,; City Colleges of Chicago, "2015 Score Card," http://www.ccc.edu/ news/Documents/DO_FY15_Scorecard.pdf; internal data.

2. Bill Gates, "Shaking Up Higher Education with Cheryl Hyman," *Gatesnotes* (blog), June 3, 2015, https://www.gatesnotes.com/Education/Shaking-Up-Higher-Education-with-Cheryl-Hyman.

3. Thomas R. Bailey, Shanna Smith Jaggars, and Davis Jenkins, *Redesigning America's Community Colleges* (Cambridge, MA: Harvard University Press, 2015), 185–188.

4. http://collegecompletion.chronicle.com/state/#state = az&sector = public_two; http://www.arizonacommunitycolleges.org/outcomes/pdf/azcc_2016_district_ outcomes_report.pdf;https://www.luminafoundation.org/files/resources/early-results-tn-es.pdf; http://www.governing.com/topics/education/gov-tennessee-free-community-college-promise.html; https://www.insidehighered.com/news/ 2014/08/26/bill-haslams-free-community-college-plan-and-how-tennessee-grabbing-spotlight-higher.

5. http://completecollege.org/college-completion-data/.

6. https://nces.ed.gov/programs/digest/d16/tables/dt16_326.20.asp.

7. For details on Valencia's approach, see Joshua S. Wyner, *What Excellent Community Colleges Do: Preparing All Students for Success* (Cambridge, MA: Harvard Education Press, 2014).

8. Fawn Johnson, "How a Community College's Big Ideas Are Transforming Education," reprinted in *The Atlantic*, October 12, 2012, https://www.theatlantic.com/ politics/archive/2012/10/how-a-community-colleges-big-ideas-are-transforming-education/429057/.

9. https://assets.aspeninstitute.org/content/uploads/files/content/docs/pubs/ AspenPrize021312.pdf, 7–10; Johnson, "How a Community College's Big Ideas Are Transforming Education."

10. Steven Strahler, "How City Colleges Inflates Graduation Rates," *Crain's*, October 17, 2015, http://www.chicagobusiness.com/article/20151017/ISSUE01/ 310179995/how-city-colleges-inflates-graduation-rates.

CHAPTER 9

1. For a useful analysis of the differing views of shared governance, see Gary A. Olson, "Exactly What Is 'Shared Governance'?" *Chronicle of Higher Education*, July 23, 2009.

2. Fran Spielman, "City Colleges chief to end stormy six year run with long goodbye," *Chicago Sun-Times*, October 17, 2015, https://chicago.suntimes.com/ news/city-colleges-chief-to-end-stormy-six-year-run-with-long-goodbye/.

3. OECD (2017), *Population with Tertiary Education* (Indicator), doi: 10.1787/ 0b8f90e9-en (accessed June 27, 2017); Mikhail Zinshteyn, "College Graduation Rates Rise, but Racial Gaps Persist and Men Still Out-Perform Women," *Hechinger Report*, May 26, 2016, http://hechingerreport.org/college-graduation-rates-rise-racial-gaps-persist-men-still-earn-women.

ACKNOWLEDGMENTS

I asked myself why I wanted—indeed, needed—to write this book. The answer came to me during one of those evenings when my brain refused to shut down and sleep eluded me.

Community colleges are a truly American invention with the potential to be amazingly valuable assets for our country. They have provided access to the middle class for millions of people and have been integral to fueling our economy over the last fifty years. However, they no longer adequately meet the education needs of so many of their students. Far too many of them have dismal rates of success, and students who earn degrees often find them to be of limited value.

To point out the current underperformance of community colleges is not necessarily to lay blame on faculty, administrators, or staff; chronic underfunding and decades of outdated strategies that have not emphasized relevance and data can make any of us products of our workplaces. However, we must break old habits so that our workplaces are a product of the dreams and needs of those they are supposed to serve: students and society at large. Students look to higher education to prepare them to get good jobs. Employers struggle with finding skilled employees to fill available, well-paying jobs. As America lags behind other nations in academic preparedness, its competitiveness suffers along with the economic prospects of individuals.

I have written this book to use the example of the Reinvention of the City Colleges of Chicago and other best-performing community colleges to shine a bright spotlight on the potential of these institutions. It also aims to serve as an inspiration and a road map for those looking to make change in the field.

Within a very short time frame, City Colleges experienced dramatically improved student outcomes—not through pursuing incremental change but through the implementation of a radical process of change. Other community colleges can achieve the same results. And if every institution tripled its number of well-trained graduates, it would fuel dramatic changes for millions of Americans—in particular, benefiting minorities, immigrants, and those of modest economic means.

This book illustrates the obstacles faced and lessons learned in attempting true large-scale reform—even revolution—of one of the largest educational institutions in the country. The educators, students, political leaders, and others who read this book will likely find parts of it disturbing, but I hope they will find other parts thought-provoking. I want it to force an open and honest dialogue and probe much more deeply into how well community colleges are really serving the people who enter their doors seeking a path to a better life. Most importantly, I hope it inspires thousands of leaders—faculty, administrators, legislators, and students—to take immediate action and implement fundamental changes at their institutions and within their state to ensure they are exclusively focused on students. Lives depend on it, and our nation depends on it.

Books can't generally be written in isolation, and my case was no exception. Let me start by looking up and thanking the good Lord. Like many others, my life has been a journey of starts and stops, ups and downs. My deep foundation in faith has helped me through every trial and tribulation I have had to face and overcome. It's very true, God doesn't send you more than you can stand, but sometimes when you are in the moment, it's difficult to accept that.

There are a number of people I want to recognize. Of course, my mom, Katherine, and dad, Robert. In overcoming the demons and daily struggles that afflict so many inner-city African American families, they taught me the meaning of perseverance and boundless determination.

To Debbie, my godsister, who's always felt like my blood sister, for providing another set of eyes and unlimited encouragement.

My two aunts Chris and Jacklyn and my uncle James for always being there for me.

The Garmon and Norsworthy families for simply loving me.

My City Colleges of Chicago leadership team, who I often refer to as my "kitchen cabinet," for their undying loyalty and superior execution, which provided the basis for much of the data used in writing this book. Their commitment to Reinvention and my vision touched my very soul.

My core of outstanding college presidents, without whose dedication and hard work my success and our student achievements wouldn't have been possible.

City Colleges of Chicago faculty, staff, and administrators, thank you for your commitment to education and the countless hours and hard work spent on the Reinvention task forces. Addressing your concerns has helped broaden my perspective and understanding of the challenges we jointly face.

My predecessors, for giving me the platform to build on.

My corporate mentors, who told me I could be a leader even when I didn't believe I could be.

My editors, Linda Perlstein and Caroline Chauncey, whom in all honesty I can't give enough credit to. This book couldn't have been completed without their critical feedback and guidance on structure and organization. More importantly, I thank them for helping me put my thoughts, ideas, and opinion in the proper perspective!

Finally I want to thank my publisher, Harvard Education Press. They believed in me and what I wanted my book to say and the accomplishments that were achieved under Reinvention.

So to everyone—a big THANK YOU.

ABOUT THE AUTHOR

As Chancellor of the City Colleges of Chicago, CHERYL HYMAN was responsible for managing a $700 million budget, overseeing fifty-five hundred employees, and ensuring the success of more than 100,000 students annually. Appointed by Mayor Richard M. Daley in 2010 and reappointed by Mayor Rahm Emanuel a year later, Hyman led the Reinvention of the City Colleges of Chicago in partnership with faculty, staff, students, four-year colleges, and members of the civic and business communities to ensure that all CCC students successfully graduated ready for further college and careers. During this time, the graduation rate more than doubled and degrees awarded annually were the highest on record in City Colleges' history. Hyman also launched College to Careers, which partners faculty and staff with more than 150 industry leaders and universities to better prepare students for careers in fast-growing fields. She oversaw a balanced budget each year of her tenure with no increase in taxes, saved $70 million, launched a $524 million capital plan, and negotiated student outcome goals into key labor agreements.

Before being appointed Chancellor, Hyman had a fourteen-year career at ComEd, an Exelon company, rising to Vice President of Operations Strategy and Business Intelligence. She served on the board of the Illinois Community College Board and now serves on the boards of Complete College America and the Chicago History Museum, is a member of the Commercial Club of Chicago and the Economic Club of Chicago, and serves as a member on the Urban Institute's US Partnership on Mobility from Poverty. She previously served as a court-appointed special advocate for children who were wards of the court, and served on the board of directors for The Night Ministry, a Chicago-based organization that works to provide housing, health care, and human connection to members of the community struggling with poverty or homelessness.

A graduate of the community college system she once ran, Hyman also holds an executive master of business administration from Northwestern University's Kellogg School of Management, a master of arts degree in community development and a certification in nonprofit management from North Park University, and a bachelor of science degree in computer science from the Illinois Institute of Technology.

INDEX

technological tools
  for scheduling, 104–105
  for student support, 101–103
technology, 40, 64–65, 76
Tennessee, 129
tenure process, 19, 55–57
third-party providers, 117
training, 31
transfer center, 103
transfer partnerships, 38, 78, 98, 100
transfer pathways, 85, 96–98
transfer students, 18, 24–25, 51, 76–82, 124
transparency, 46
transportation, distribution, and logistics (TDL) programs, 66–67, 81–82, 85–87
Truman, Harry S., 15
Truman College, 87, 88
tuition, 106–108, 135
tuition revenue, 59
tutoring centers, 103

University of Chicago, 13, 14
University of Illinois, 78, 96–97, 100

Valencia College, 38, 56, 130–132
veteran support center, 103
vocational education, 69–70, 72–73, 77–78

website, 64, 101
wellness center, 103
White House Summit on Community Colleges, 20–21
whole-program enrollment, 105, 143
whole-school reform, 17–27, 33–34
  See also Reinvention of City Colleges of Chicago
Wilbur Wright College, 87
Women Employed, 118
workforce advisory groups, 75–76
workforce development team, 92
workplace skills, 5, 17, 69–92
work schedules, 105
Wright College, 114–115, 134
Wyner, Josh, 74

zero-based budgeting, 62